THE PERSONAL TRAINER BUSINESS HANDBOOK

by *Ed Gaut*

Willow Creek Publications

Published by **Willow Creek Publications**
A division of Gaucas, Inc.
P.O. Box 86032
Gaithersburg, MD 20886

This publication is designed to provide accurate and authoritative information in regard to the subject matter covered. It is sold with the understanding that the publisher is not engaged in rendering legal, accounting, or other professional service. If legal advice or other expert assistance is required, the services of a competent professional person should be sought. *From a Declaration of Principles jointly adopted by a Committee of the American Bar Association and a Committee of Publishers.*

ISBN: 0-9640945-3-3
Library of Congress Catalog Card Number: 94-060172

Table of Contents

Acknowledgement

A book by a first-time author, whose area of expertise is exercise and fitness —not writing—is by necessity a collaboration; this is no exception. During the writing of the book, I was fortunate enough to have the help of a number of people who gave generously of their time and talents. I would in particular like to thank Marla Footer and Michele DeNinno, successful personal trainers, who reviewed some of the early drafts and provided valuable encouragement and advice. I also would like to thank Dorothea Garber Cracas. Her insightful comments and suggestions regarding both style and substance have been incorporated in many places, and the book is better for them. I also would like to thank Becky Hines who proofread the final draft. Her eye for detail and good sense have saved me from more than one embarrassing mistake. And finally, I would like to thank David Cracas, the publisher of Willow Creek Publications. It was David who initially suggested this project several years ago. It was David who shepherded it through numerous drafts. And it was David whose enthusiasm kept the project going when, from time to time, my enthusiasm waned. If this book is a success, it is due in large part to his efforts.

Chapter One
Becoming a Personal Trainer

1.1 Why Become an Independent Personal Trainer

I am riding along in my Jeep, top down, enjoying the day. It is a sunny, warm spring morning with a clear, blue sky, the kind of morning when no one should be inside. Most commuters are at work by now, and I have the road to myself. Casually dressed in a short sleeve shirt and shorts, I probably look like a college student cutting classes for the day to head to the beach. In reality, I am at work, have been since 5 a.m. when I knocked on the door of my first client. It is now 10 o'clock, and I have already trained four clients and am on my way to a local gym to train another.

My name is Ed Gaut. I am a personal trainer and owner of a personal training company, Bodies Plus Fitness Systems. My company provides fitness related services in the Washington, D.C. area: one-on-one personal training, personalized nutrition counseling, group aerobics programs—we do it all. In fact, we are one of the fastest growing personal training companies in the country.

Seven years ago, having an interest in fitness and not finding a job that suited my talents, I decided to create my own job. So I founded Bodies Plus Fitness Systems. At first I worked alone. But little by little, the business has grown, and today I employ other trainers to assist me.

Now you might think that dressing casually, keeping your own hours, spending your days in gyms and health clubs, and owning your own business is a nice life, and it is. But that is not why I do what I do. For me, these are just perks, advantages of the job. The most important reasons for running my own personal training business are much deeper.

Basically, the reason I am doing what I do is that I love the fitness field. I love working with people to improve the quality of their lives. And I love being around other people involved with fitness.

Picture a typical client of mine, a middle-aged woman. She has not exercised since she was a teenager and she is overweight. Perhaps her husband or mother-in-law has started making comments about her appearance. Perhaps her doctor has told her that her blood pressure is too high and she needs to do something about it. Perhaps an energetic friend has recommended that she try exercising to increase her energy level. Or perhaps she is no longer happy with what she sees in the mirror and finally has decided to take action. Whatever the reasons, she comes to me.

In a matter of months—weeks even—we can transform her life. Several times a week we work out together. At first she is clumsy, perhaps a little hesitant. She gets frustrated easily; progress seems nonexistent. But slowly, imperceptibly, week by week, changes are taking place. Fat is being replaced by muscle. Fatigue and depression are being replaced by energy and a new confidence. Suddenly her husband is noticing that she is taking better care of herself, her mother-in-law is complimenting her on her figure, and she is excited by the changes she sees in the mirror. Best of all, she is on her way to living a longer, healthier life.

Now, I am not God. I did not make these changes happen. She did. But I helped her make them happen. I facilitated them. Without me she would still be looking in the mirror, making excuses.

I was there with her every step of the way, coaching, cajoling, praising, sometimes criticizing. I was there when she

first started out, when her goals seemed impossibly far away. I was there the days she was depressed and did not want to go on. And I was there the day she was so excited because she noticed the first changes in her body.

This is exciting stuff, being able to make such a significant contribution to peoples' lives, watching as an overweight woman becomes lean and trim or as a skinny teenager gets bigger and stronger. Ultimately, that is what the personal training business is all about. It is about helping people to live longer, healthier, happier lives. And that is why I do what I do.

Now, that may not excite you. I hope it does, but it may not. You may have other reasons for wanting to start your own personal training business.

Perhaps you are already working as a trainer in a gym or health club. If so, you probably are making $10 to $15 per hour while the club takes in three to four times that. You have no control over which clients you train or when you train them. Even worse, when you are not training clients, you are more than likely folding towels and cleaning equipment.

Or perhaps you are not in the fitness field yet. Perhaps you are working some nine-to-five job in an office or behind a fast food counter. Every day you have the same routine; you drive to work in the morning, put in your time, and drive home at night. The next day, you do the same thing.

You may see starting your own

personal training business as a way to get control over your work and your time, to decide what you are going to do and when you are going to do it. You may see it as a way to make more money from the work you do. Or you may see it as a way to make work more fun. These are all valid reasons, and if you are willing to do what it takes, starting your own personal training business offers these opportunities as well.

1.2 What it Takes to be a Personal Trainer

Running your own personal training business can be very rewarding and you can earn a lot of money doing it. The bad news, however, is that it is not as easy as it looks. If you are already in the business, you know that. If not, consider what it will take to be an independent personal trainer.

1.2.1 A Knowledge of Exercise and Fitness

It should be obvious that the first requirement for running your own personal training business is having a knowledge of exercise and fitness. If you do not, you will not get very far. I guarantee it. You can only fake it so long. New clients will want to see credentials and references from other clients, and this is very much a business built on word of mouth. If you do not know what you are doing, clients will

figure this out, and they will tell their friends.

In addition, if you start training clients without having the necessary knowledge and skills, you will not be able to train them effectively or safely. This means that at best you will be cheating them, and at worst, injuring them. This is bad for the clients, bad for you, and bad for the personal training business in general.

Most of you reading this probably are thinking that what I have just said does not apply to you. After all, you probably have some familiarity with exercise and fitness—you undoubtedly work out yourself, perhaps you are even training other people. You may think you already know enough about exercise and fitness to run a personal training business. This may or may not be the case.

If you have no formal education or training in exercise and fitness, I strongly suggest that you take some courses before starting your business. If nothing else, this will confirm that you know what you need to know and provide you with credentials to show prospective clients.

1.2.2 A Suitable Personality

Other than being knowledgeable about exercise and fitness, probably the most important requirement for being a successful personal trainer is having the right personality. Since your ultimate goal is to get and keep clients, your personality, your ability to interact with others, is crucial to your success.

First, this means that you must be what my grandmother would call a "go getter." Especially in the beginning, you must be willing to go out there and do whatever it takes to get business: making cold calls to prospective clients, writing letters to newspapers and magazines, approaching people in gyms and health clubs. You must be ready and willing to jump in. At first, business will not come to you; you must go in search of it.

It is not easy, believe me. When you are first starting out, every spare moment you have you will need to spend promoting your business. You cannot sit around on your *gluteus maximus* if you want to be successful. So, if you are shy or introverted, running your own personal training business is probably not for you.

In addition to being outgoing and somewhat aggressive, having the right personality to be a personal trainer also means you must be a good leader. This means that you must be able to motivate your clients without alienating them. You must be able to maintain control without being overbearing. And, you must be knowledgeable about exercise and fitness, yet be able to express your knowledge in a way that does not annoy clients.

Many of your clients, for example, will be professionals such as doctors and lawyers. These are people who are accustomed to being the ones to whom other people come for help. As a rule, they do not take kindly to advice or criticism. You will need a great deal of tact and patience to deal with them.

Having the right personality also means you must be diplomatic and encouraging. It takes a while for new clients who have not previously exercised to become accustomed to working out. They will not be familiar with the exercises or the muscle soreness which occurs after exercising. This can cause them to become despondent and discouraged, perhaps even quit after just a few sessions. You have to be prepared to deal with this, to encourage them without being overly-solicitous.

As a trainer, you will have to be ready to deal with the whole client, not just his or her body. This means dealing on a day-to-day basis with other people's idiosyncrasies and problems. You would be amazed what clients will say to you once you become a regular part of their lives. I know things about clients that even their spouses do not know. This requires a certain amount of tact, particularly if you train both husband and wife.

Finally, as a personal trainer, you must be observant and a good listener. Clients will not always tell you what they are feeling. You must be ready to sense what they are feeling from what they do and how they act. In other words, you must have what psychologists call good "body awareness skills."

Every now and then, for example, I get a client, usually a man, who has a macho attitude and does not want to let me know how hard he is truly working during a workout. He would rather die than admit a weight is too heavy or the aerobic music too fast. If I am not paying close attention, I could easily push him too far, risking injury. In this type of situation, it is essential to be extremely observant.

Even when being honest, a client may not be knowledgeable enough to express concerns he or she may have in a way that I can understand. A common problem with inexperienced clients is the evaluation of potential injuries. For example, a client may have a serious injury but neglect to mention it.

A client also may have a minor ache which he or she describes as a major problem. Soft tissue injuries, for example, generally need to be treated with exercise. This increases blood circulation to the injury and aids healing. It means, however, working out with some pain. It may be difficult for a client to understand this, that a certain level of discomfort is a normal part of recovery and is okay.

This is the bottom line: being a successful personal trainer—particularly if you are running your own personal training business—means more than just knowing about exercise. It means knowing about people and how to deal with them, and it means having a suitable personality. You may be very knowledgeable about exercise and fitness, but if you are shy and introverted, if you are quick-tempered or impatient, or if you are not very observant, you probably are not going to be successful running your own personal training business.

1.2.3 A Healthy Lifestyle

In addition to a suitable personality, in order to succeed as a personal trainer, you need to live a healthy lifestyle. This means that you must be physically fit and be willing to practice what you preach. You do not have to have a fantastic physique, but you cannot be an overweight, fat slob. Remember, you are your own best advertisement. If you do not look like you know anything about fitness, you are not going to attract many clients.

It should be obvious that this means you cannot smoke or drink in front of clients. If you do have some unhealthy habits—and who does not—you had better not let clients see them. Do as I say and not as I do will only work so long. As a personal trainer you are a role model, especially for younger clients.

While I am on the subject of lifestyle and unhealthy habits, let me say something about steroids and personal training. I know there are people who use anabolic steroids. As far as I am concerned, that is their business. If they are willing to take the risks—both physical and, increasingly, legal—that is up to them. I can understand why they do it even if I do not agree with it. But it creates a problem when a steroid user is also a personal trainer.

Now you might think that using steroids would be an advantage for a personal trainer. After all, you may figure, if you have a bodybuilder's physique, people will assume you must know what you are doing. Who would not want you as a personal trainer?

There is some truth to this; there will be some clients who are attracted by a huge, heavily-muscled personal trainer. But there also will be many potential clients who will feel intimidated and uncomfortable with a personal trainer who has a steroid body and the attitude which frequently accompanies it.

Remember, the majority of your clients are not going to be like your friends from the gym. They are going to be well-to-do, middle-aged men and women. When they choose a personal trainer, they will be looking for someone they feel comfortable with, someone they can invite into their homes and their lives on a regular basis. A fit, attractive person, not a steroid freak, is nine times out of ten what they will be looking for.

Steroid use also presents another even more serious problem for a personal trainer. As I said before, a personal trainer is a role model. Use of steroids will not pose much of a problem when training a middle-aged woman who wants to lose a few pounds. The last thing she is looking for is to bulk up. Use of steroids, however, will be a problem when training a young, male client—for example, a kid who wants to get bigger for football or just to impress his friends. No matter what the trainer says, the kid is going to get the message that the way to get big is to use drugs. If

the personal trainer is not only using steroids himself, but selling them as well, it is even more of a problem.

As far as I am concerned, the use of steroids is not compatible with being a personal trainer. I realize, however, that some of you reading this are using them. As I said, that is your business. Just be sure to keep them to yourself. Remember, you are a personal trainer, not a drug pusher.

1.2.4 Running Your Own Business

Someone once asked the millionaire banker Andrew Mellon what the secret to success in business is. He replied that the secret is to only work half a day, and he added, it does not matter whether you work the first half or the second half. What he meant, of course, is that if you are going to be successful, you are probably going to be putting in twelve-hour days. If this were ever true of any business, it is certainly true of the personal training business.

Some businesses, manufacturing for instance, are capital intensive; they require a lot of money to get off the ground. The personal training business is not one of those. Fortunately, it can be started with a minimal investment of money. It does, however, require a lot of labor, what entrepreneurs call "sweat equity." This means an investment of personal time and energy.

I started Bodies Plus Fitness Systems seven years ago. For the first year or so,

I worked seven days a week, nine to twelve hours a day. Today, seven years later, I still work a six-day week, often getting up at five in the morning and working through until nine or ten at night. If I am not training clients, I am managing the other trainers who work for me, getting new clients, generating publicity, and dealing with the endless other details involved in running a business.

The point is just this: if you want a nine-to-five job, work for someone else. If you are going to start your own personal training business, you had better be prepared to work long hours. You also had better be prepared to manage your own business. This might not seem like much of a problem, but of all the things that I have had to do to be successful, I have found this to be one of the hardest. Managing a business includes keeping financial records, paying taxes, and eventually managing employees. It also requires knowing something about marketing or at least being willing to learn.

Take me for example. I am knowledgeable about health and fitness, I am outgoing and have no trouble dealing with new people and new situations, and I am not afraid of long hours and hard work. But keeping my business organized has always been a real challenge. Believe me, the last thing you want to do upon returning home at ten o'clock at night after dragging a three hundred pound woman through a fifty-minute workout is to post income or pay bills.

Time was when every piece of information I needed for my business was scribbled on separate scraps of paper somewhere in my apartment. I could never clean for fear I would throw away something important. It goes without saying that tax time was a nightmare; my accountant would run whenever he saw me coming. Fortunately, being in top shape, I was faster and could usually catch him.

As my business grew, however, I realized that this was just not going to work, and eventually I got my act together. Today, I have things more under control. I have a filing system which I generally use. I keep on top of the paper work. And my accountant now usually returns my calls.

In all seriousness, here is the point: if you are going to run your own personal training business, you are going to have to manage it. This is boring and time-consuming. Believe me, I know. But, you have to do it. As I said before, the alternative is to work for someone else.

1.3 About This Book

If you already are running your own personal training business, the above information should not be news to you. You already know what it takes. In the following chapters, you will find ideas on how to improve and expand your business—how, for example, to get more clients or start group programs. Since you already are in business, you may want to skip around and read those topics and chapters that interest you.

If, on the other hand, you are just starting or thinking of starting your own personal training business, what I have said so far should not come as a shock to you. You probably already had some idea what running your own personal training business would take. In the rest of the book, you will find a step-by-step guide to get you started.

Chapter II, *Training and Credentials*, describes the various types of education, training, and certification programs available for personal trainers. In it, you will find suggestions on what you need and what you do not need. This will help ensure that you have the necessary training and credentials without spending unnecessary money.

Chapter III, *Setting Up Your Business*, provides a step-by-step guide to setting up your personal training business. It deals with issues such as creating a business plan; choosing a type of business; obtaining licenses, permits, and insurance; and dealing with bookkeeping and taxes. This chapter is essential if you are just starting your business.

Chapter IV, *Getting Clients*, describes the three most effective techniques for getting and keeping new clients. It also discusses what to do once you get a client. If you are just starting out, this chapter will provide an invaluable guide to getting your first client. If you are already in the business, you will find ideas here to increase your clientele.

Chapter V, *Getting into Gyms and Health Clubs*, describes how to become associated with a gym or health club as an outside trainer. Doing this will dramatically increase your access to new clients, provide you with free publicity, and add another item to your list of credentials. This chapter tells you how.

Chapter VI, *Advertising and Publicity*, is a guide to getting your business known. It includes information on generating free publicity as well as advertising with flyers, direct mail, and in local periodicals. It also includes information on promotional ideas such as gift certificates and coupons.

Chapter VII, *Expanding Your Business*, discusses how to expand your business beyond your own one-on-one personal training. It includes information on hiring other trainers and creating group programs. If you are already running your own personal training business and are looking for ideas to expand it, you will want to read this chapter.

The goal of this book is to provide you with the information you need to start and run a successful personal training business. I am a personal trainer, not a writer. In spite of this, I hope that I accomplish my goal and that you find this book valuable. I realize my limitations, however, and am always looking for advice. I welcome any comments or suggestions you might have.

Chapter Two
Training and Credentials

Before you start your personal training business, you will need to know enough about exercise and fitness to train clients safely and effectively. If you do not already have the necessary knowledge and skills, you will need to remedy this either through formal education or exercise and fitness training programs. Even if you already have the skills and the know-how to train clients, you still will need to take some certification programs to give yourself the necessary credentials.

If you start training clients without having the necessary knowledge and skills, you will not get very far. The personal training business is built on word of mouth. Many, if not most, of your clients will come by way of referrals from other clients, and those who do not will almost always want references from other clients. If you get a reputation for not knowing what you are doing or worse, injuring people, you will not last very long.

In the Washington, D.C. area where I train, there are too many so-called personal trainers with absolutely no education or formal training in exercise and fitness. Their credentials consist only of five-cent business cards naming them as personal trainers. I reiterate, if you have no formal training, I strongly suggest you take some courses before starting your business, even if you believe you already have the necessary knowledge and fitness experience. If nothing else, this will provide you with credentials that you can show prospective clients.

2.1 Education and Training

Education and training in exercise and fitness can be obtained through college degree programs, personal training courses and seminars, and on-the-job opportunities in health clubs and personal training companies, as well as through self-study materials such as books and periodicals. The options you choose will depend upon your current level of knowledge and the amount of time and money you can afford to spend.

2.1.1 Education

While it certainly is not necessary to have a college degree in order to work as a personal trainer, if you want to separate yourself from all the people calling themselves personal trainers— and as I said before, there are a lot of these people out there—you must have a degree. Prospective clients will ask about degrees and education. In my experience, only about one-third of all personal trainers have a college degree in a fitness related field. For that reason, even if your degree is a two-year associate's degree, having a degree in a fitness-related field will put you ahead of 60% to 70% of all the people claiming to be personal trainers. In addition, you will need a degree if you want to obtain certification from any of the more reputable fitness organizations, since most require a degree as a prerequisite for enrollment.

If you earn a degree, it should obviously be in a fitness-related field such as kinesiology, physical education, or physical therapy. Even a degree in dance can be useful. Any field that imparts a general understanding of how the human body works will be an advantage to you as a personal trainer.

2.1.2 Training

In addition to a formal college education, there are many other ways to receive training in exercise and fitness. One of the best ways is through courses offered by organizations such as the American College of Sports Medicine (ACSM), the Aerobics and Fitness Association of America (AFAA), IDEA, the National Sports Performance Association (NSPA), and the National Strength Conditioning Association (NSCA).

Taking one of these practical personal training courses is a good idea even if you have a college degree in an exercise and fitness related field. Being a good personal trainer means more than just knowing about the science of exercise and fitness. It means knowing how to train clients safely and effectively, which is something that cannot be learned in a classroom. Many of the things you need to know seem simple, almost obvious, but knowing them can mean the difference between an effective, safe workout and serious injury.

Another way to gain practical experience as a personal trainer is to work for a gym or health club. This has the advantage that, rather than paying money, you are earning money while gaining general exposure. Do not expect too much formal training doing this, however. Working for a gym or health club should be considered an addition, not an alternative, to formal training. Do not expect to be paid very well either. However, even if you do not learn very much or make very much money, this experience will be a valuable addition to your list of credentials.

Another option for college students

wanting to gain experience as a personal trainer is to intern with a personal training company. Companies such as mine are usually eager to take in college interns. We view them as a potential source of future employees and, to be perfectly honest, cheap labor. If you intern with a good company, you should learn a lot about both exercise and fitness and the business of being a personal trainer. As with gyms and health clubs, however, do not expect to be paid very well.

The way to start an internship is to first approach a personal training firm and offer your services. Obviously, the more knowledge of exercise and fitness you have, the better. You do not have to be an expert—after all, that is why you want to do the internship. But you do need to have enthusiasm and a willingness to learn.

Once you have made arrangements with a personal training company, get in touch with the physical education department at your college or university to arrange to earn credit for your internship. The school may or may not agree to do this. Even without obtaining college credit, however, the internship is still worthwhile just for the experience you will gain.

Let me give you one word of warning when entering into an internship: be wary of employment contracts with noncompetition clauses known as non-compete agreements. When you are hired, the personal training company will want you to sign a contract in which you agree not to compete with the company for business. This is fair as long as it is restricted to the duration of your employment and to the company's clients. Anything which restricts you from training clients after you leave the company's employment, other than restrictions on training that particular company's clients, should be avoided. Remember, you do not want to sign anything which might interfere with starting your own business or working for another company later.

Remember that employment contracts and non-compete agreements are negotiable. So, if the contract does not meet your needs, insist that the company change it. Be prepared to haggle a little and, if necessary, walk away. If you are going to run your own personal training business, you will need to become comfortable negotiating contracts. You might as well start now.

2.1.3 Reading

An effective and inexpensive form of education and training is reading. There are many excellent books, periodicals, and videos available on subjects of interest to personal trainers. However, everyone and his uncle is writing a book or doing a video on exercise and fitness today. So, along with good advice, there is a lot of bad advice. Keep an open mind, but do not believe everything you read or hear.

In addition, be aware of what your clients are reading. I have several female clients who read *Vogue* and *Cosmopolitan*, for example. You may not be aware of it—I was not—but these fashion magazines contain fitness-related articles. Clients will often read something in one of these magazines and want my opinion of it.

Similarly, you may have a teenage client come to you with a new exercise routine he just read about in a muscle magazine such as *Flex* or a female client come to you with a new diet she just read about in a fitness magazine such as *Shape*. You certainly do not need to subscribe to or read all these magazines. But you need to be aware of what is out there and, if necessary, be prepared to get a copy and discuss it with your client.

The fact that clients are looking for other sources of information should not be viewed as an inconvenience or threat to your position, but rather as part of the training process. Clients should be encouraged to learn more about exercise and fitness. At the same time, you need to impress upon them that just because something is in print does not mean it is true. You need to be prepared to tell them when you believe that something they have read or heard is misleading. In the end, this process not only educates your clients, but forces you to stay current as well.

2.1.4 Continuing Education

With advances in communication and information technology the world of

---

List of Education and Certification Organizations for Personal Trainers

Aerobics and Fitness Association of America (AFAA) (800) 446-2322

American Council on Exercise (ACE) (800) 825-3636

American College of Sports Medicine (ACSM) (317) 637-9200

Exercise Safety Association (ESA) (800) 622-7233

IDEA (800) 999-4332 ext. 7

National Sports Performance Association (NSPA) (301) 428-2879

National Strength Conditioning Association (NSCA) (402) 476-6669

---

ideas is changing ever more quickly. This is as true of exercise and fitness as it is of any other field. New training concepts, diets, and equipment are constantly being developed; old ideas are being discarded. For a personal trainer, it means that to stay on top of the field you need to be learning constantly.

This does not mean you need to be taking courses perpetually, which would be impractical as well as prohibitively expensive. However, you need to be reading and looking for new ideas on a regular basis. You also should be prepared to go back occasionally and take a new course or two. Some of the better certification programs, such as those mentioned later in this chapter, encourage this by requiring you to take a certain number of credits to maintain your certification.

2.2 Certification Programs

As the demand for personal trainers has grown, so has the need for certification programs. In response, numerous organizations have sprung up in the last few years offering programs. There are now several hundred different organizations in the United States that certify personal trainers. Some of these programs are good; most are not. Unfortunately, many are set up by enterprising individuals and organizations simply as a way to cash in on the demand and to make money.

2.2.1 Choosing a Certification Program

The two oldest and most respected organizations with certification programs applicable to personal trainers are the American College of Sports Medicine (ACSM) and the National Strength and Conditioning Association (NSCA). The ASCM offers three certification programs: Exercise Leader, Health/Fitness Director, and Health/Fitness Instructor. The NSCA offers two certification programs: Certified Strength and Conditioning Specialist and Certified Personal Trainer. The Certified Strength and Conditioning Specialist program focuses on team coaching.

When choosing a program, there are a number of things to look for. Check the pass rate of the program, which is the percentage of people taking the program who successfully pass. If it is high, 90% or more, the program probably is not very rigorous. Check if the program has a practical, hands-on examination. Again, if it has only a written test, it probably is not very rigorous. Finally, check the prerequisites required by the program. The better programs, such as those offered by the ACSM and the NSCA, require CPR and recommend a college degree in a related field or equivalent knowledge in order to enroll.

While clients will ask if you are certified, they probably will not know the difference between a good and a bad certification program. All the programs, after all, have impressive sounding names. However, although clients will probably not know the difference, fitness managers in health clubs and gyms may. Being certified by a reputable organization could mean the difference between being able and not being able to train clients in a local gym. More importantly, though, becoming certified by a good organization assures that you know what you are doing, thereby providing your clients with the best possible training.

I suggest that you obtain at least one certification before starting your personal training business. The table in this chapter provides names and telephone numbers of some of the more reputable organizations. Call up and get information on the programs that interest you.

If you already have some type of certification, you are all set. If not, you do not need to run out and take every certification program available. Get certified under one program to get started. Then add other certifications later.

2.2.2 *The Cost of Certification Programs*

Certification programs cost anywhere from $100 to $1000. The more expensive programs include training. If you do not have the necessary knowledge and hands-on experience, you will want to take one of the programs which offers hands-on training. If, however, you already have practical experience, it is much less expensive to take a program that does not include practical training.

2.3 *Tax Deduction for Education and Certification*

One of the advantages of running a business and working for yourself is that business expenses, such as the cost of education and certification programs, as well as books and periodicals, are tax deductible. This means you will save about one third of the cost, depending on the rate at which you or your business is taxed. Remember to take this into account when figuring out how much you can afford to spend on education and training.

Chapter Three
Setting up Your Business

You have decided to become an independent personal trainer. You are already knowledgeable about exercise and fitness or have gotten the necessary education and training. You may have even acquired some clients or at least have some prospective clients in mind. Before you start training, however, you need to take some time to set up your business. Being a personal trainer is a very busy life. Take the time now, while you have it, to set up your business correctly. Then, once you are organized, you can concentrate on training clients, without constantly worrying about administrative details.

3.1 A Business Plan

It is somewhat trite, but nonetheless true, that you will never get anywhere in this world unless you decide where it is you want to go and how you intend to get there. A business plan is a map for your business that does just this. For large businesses, which require outside investors or bank loans, a business plan is a formal document. For your pur-poses, however, it can be anything from a typewritten proposal to some hand-written notes. The point is this: whatever it consists of, you need to have a plan.

The discussion below should provide you with enough information to create an informal business plan which will be sufficient for your personal training business. If you want to go beyond this and develop a formal business plan, there are many excellent books devoted entirely to the subject. Check with local bookstores and libraries.

As you prepare your business plan, remember that it will not be etched in stone. It can and will change as your business evolves. In fact, once created, your business plan should be reviewed and updated regularly.

3.1.1 Objectives and Goals

The first element of your business plan should be a brief description of your business objective and goals. Why are you starting this business—to make more money or to provide yourself with a more flexible schedule? How much money do you want to make? Do you intend to remain a one-man shop or would you like to eventually hire employees? Where do you want the business to be in six months, in a year, in five years?

Your goals and objectives may or may not be realistic. You probably cannot tell at this point. Writing down your objectives and goals will at least give you a clearer idea of what they are. Then, as you start running your business and get some experience under your belt, you can review your goals and, if necessary, revise them.

3.1.2 *Target Customers and Services*

The second element of your business plan should be a definition of your target customers and the services you intend to offer them. Understanding who your customers are and what you are trying to sell them will affect all aspects of your business from how and where you advertise to what you name your company. Things to consider when defining your customers include: age, sex, social class, income level, profession, goals and interests.

You might decide, for example, that you want to target middle-aged women who are looking for weight loss and toning. Or you might have an interest in bodybuilding and want to train men and women interested in building muscle. Or you might want to teach step or water aerobics to teenagers.

Whatever types of clients you choose, remember to consider the area you will be working in and the kinds of people in that area who will be willing and able to pay for your services. Realistically, most of your clients will be middle-class or wealthy. While it might be very satisfying to improve the lives of homeless men and women by training them at a local YMCA, if they are your only source of income, you too could wind up homeless.

3.1.3 *The Competition*

Once you have chosen the services you will offer and to whom you will offer them, take a moment to consider who is your competition. Your competitors are personal trainers and personal training companies in the same area who are offering the same types of services to the same customers as you are. A description of the competition and how you intend to deal with them should be included in your business plan.

If you are very lucky or have made your choice of location and clients well, you initially may have no competition. If so, enjoy this situation while you can. You can bet that others will follow in your footsteps soon enough.

More than likely, though, there already will be other individuals and companies in your area offering services similar to yours. Do not worry about every Tom, Dick, and Harry who has a business card which says he or she is a personal trainer. There are always a lot of these people; most go out of business pretty quickly when they discover that running a personal training business is not just a matter of knowing a barbell from a dumbbell.

You want to concern yourself with established personal trainers, individuals and companies who have been in business for awhile and who have a number of clients. If a company has been at it for at least two or three years, it probably means that the company is doing something right; you want to find out what that is.

To identify these companies and individuals, talk to the owners and managers of gyms in your area. If you are not already friendly with local gym owners, get friendly; they will be an invaluable source of information and business. Ask the owners who the big personal training companies and personal trainers in the area are.

Also, check with health clubs in the area. Call up the clubs, tell them that you are interested in training with a personal trainer, and see whom they recommend. They may refer you to inside staff, but they also may suggest an outside trainer or company. If a gym or health club recommends an outside trainer to you, it means that trainer or company has some sort of credibility in the area and is worth considering as your competition. It probably also means that the club uses outside personal trainers. So keep the club in mind when you go looking for places in which to train clients. See Chapter V, *Getting into*

Gyms and Health Clubs, for more information on how to do this.

Of course you will want to look in the Yellow Pages for any personal trainers listed and investigate any flyers, brochures, and business cards posted by personal trainers at local gyms and health clubs. As I said before, though, just because some individual or company claims to be in the personal training business, does not mean he or she is your competition. Find out more about the personal trainers whose literature you see before you add them to your list of competitors.

Once you have identified the competition, study them carefully. Ask yourself what types of customers do they target, what services do they provide, how much do they charge, and how do they market their services?

If you want to engage in a little espionage, call up—or better yet have someone else call up—the personal trainers you have identified as potential competition. Find out what they offer and how much they charge. To determine how well-established they are, ask them how long they have been in business, how many clients they have, and whether or not they can provide references from existing clients. All these are reasonable questions for a potential client to ask and, unless you act suspiciously, you should get the answers you want.

If you want to be successful, you will need to differentiate yourself from your competition. Once you know who they are and what they are doing, you can differentiate yourself from your competition in a number of ways.

One of the best ways to make yourself and your business stand out is to provide your customers with more value than the competition. Many personal trainers I have seen treat their clients like children, as if the clients were incapable of doing anything for themselves. They tell the client what to do and what not to do, never explaining or providing any additional information. Perhaps they fear that if they tell the client too much, the client will become independent and not need them anymore or perhaps they do not really care about the client.

In contrast, I like to educate my clients. I do not just tell them what to do and what not to do; I tell them why. I do not want them to follow me blindly; I want them to learn. I encourage my clients to ask questions, to seek outside sources of information, and to take charge of their own health and fitness.

This may seem of little consequence, but it is not. I take the time to educate my clients. I do it because I want to, not because it is a good marketing ploy, but the result is the same; I provide my clients with more value and that, in turn, sets me apart from my competition.

Another way to differentiate yourself from the competition is to provide unique services not otherwise available. For example, several years ago, when I first started group aerobics programs in the Washington, D.C. area, there were a number of other personal training firms already offering aerobics. I could have tried to compete head-on. Instead, I offered step aerobics, which at the time no other personal training company in the area provided. I differentiated Bodies Plus Fitness Systems from other companies in the area by offering clients something unique which they could not get anywhere else. Today, everyone is offering step aerobics classes so, although I still have a significant part of the market, I am expanding with slide aerobics and other types of new aerobics programs.

One word of warning: whatever you do, avoid competing on price. It may be tempting, especially in the beginning, to charge less than the competition in order to attract clients. Avoid this temptation. Unless you have some special advantage which makes providing services to clients less expensive for you than for your competition, this method is rarely effective for very long. Let WalMart compete on price. You compete on value. In the personal training business, where clients shop for personal trainers based on quality as much as price, charging too little or less than the going rate, can make you look cheap and leave potential clients suspicious of your abilities.

For many clients, having a personal trainer is a sign of prestige, like having an expensive automobile or fur coat. It is something to brag about to friends at the club. There are limits to this of course; no matter how wealthy, everyone wants value for his or her dollar, and if the value of your services does not warrant the fee you charge, you are not going to get or keep clients. But, just as you should be wary of pricing yourself too high, you also should avoid pricing yourself too low just to beat the competition. To a certain extent, the more expensive the personal trainer is, the more prestigious the client appears.

3.1.4 Marketing Plan

Once you have decided who your clients are, what services you will offer them, and what the competition is doing, you need to consider how to market your services. Questions to answer include what kinds of places do your target customers frequent and to what types of advertisements and publicity will they respond?

If, for example, you have decided that your clients will be middle-aged women interested in weight loss, you might choose to advertise by distributing flyers at local beauty salons, women's organizations, and other places women frequent. These flyers would be geared to women's concerns stressing weight loss, toning, and trimming.

On the other hand, if you are planning to train men and women interested in bodybuilding, you probably would want to put up flyers in local gyms. These flyers obviously would be different from the ones targeting women interested in toning and trimming; these flyers would stress weight gain rather than weight loss, for example.

Chapter IV, *Getting Clients*, and Chapter VI, *Advertising and Publicity*, discuss in detail various marketing tools and techniques you will want to consider when drawing up your business plan.

3.1.5 Estimating Income

The next element in your business plan should be an estimate of the amount of gross income you intend to generate from your business. To do this, you need to estimate the number of clients you will train each month, the number of sessions these clients will generate, and how much you intend to charge per session. Remember to be realistic about travel time, personal time, and your ability, at least in the beginning, to get clients. Assuming that your average commute between clients is no more than half an hour and that you spend an hour with each client, realistically you probably cannot train more than eight to ten clients a day—and that would be a very long day.

Worksheets for estimated income, expenses, and profits are provided in the Forms Section of this book. Since you will want to revise these Worksheets periodically, you may want to make several photocopies of each before using them. In addition to the blank worksheets, sample completed worksheets for an imaginary personal training business are provided in this chapter as examples.

Use the income worksheet to estimate

Sample Income Worksheet

	1	2	3	4	5	6	7	8	9	10	11	12
Number of clients	0	2	4	6	8	10	12	14	16	16	16	16
Number of sessions per week per client	2	2	2	2	2	2	2	2	2	2	2	2
Number of sessions per week	0	4	8	12	16	20	24	28	32	32	32	32
Number of weeks per month	4	4	4	4	4	4	4	4	4	4	4	4
Number of sessions per month	0	16	32	48	64	80	96	112	128	128	128	128
Fee per session	$ 60	$ 60	$ 60	$ 60	$ 60	$ 60	$ 60	$ 60	$ 60	$ 60	$ 60	$ 60
Gross income per month	$ 0	$ 960	$ 1,920	$ 2,880	$ 3,840	$ 4,880	$ 5,760	$ 6,720	$ 7,680	$ 7,680	$ 7,680	$ 7,680
Total gross income												$57,600

your monthly income for the first year of your business. In the first row of the income worksheet, put the number of clients you intend to train during each of the twelve months. In the sample worksheet, for example, we assume that we are starting the business with no clients and picking up two clients per month until we have a total of sixteen clients in the ninth month. The number of clients then remains constant at sixteen for the rest of the year. If finding two new clients per month seems like a very conservative estimate, remember that we primarily will be looking for quality clients who want to train with us on a permanent basis at least once per week.

In the second row of the worksheet put the average number of sessions per week you will train each client. This will vary from client to client. In the sample worksheet, we assume an average of two sessions per week. This does not mean that all or even any of our clients train twice per week. We may have some clients whom we train three or four times per week, others we train only once per week, and perhaps a few we train once or twice per month.

In the third row of the worksheet put the total number of sessions per week you will be working during each of the twelve months. This number is calculated by multiplying the number of clients in the first row by the average number of sessions per client in the second row.

The fourth row contains the number of weeks per month. For simplicity we assume four. This will give us a somewhat conservative estimate of the number of sessions per month, but that is okay. It takes into account the fact that clients inevitably get sick or go on vacation.

In the fifth row of the worksheet put the total number of sessions you will be working per month for each of twelve months. This number is calculated by multiplying the number of sessions per week in the third row by the number of weeks per month in the fourth row.

In the sixth row, put the fee per session you plan to charge. How to determine your fee is covered in Chapter IV, *Getting Clients*. In the seventh row, put the total gross income you will earn per month for each of the twelve months. This number is calculated by multiplying the number of sessions per month in the fifth row by your fee per session in the sixth row.

Finally, in the eighth row, put your total gross income for the year. This number is calculated by adding up the gross income for each month from the seventh row.

3.1.6 Estimating Expenses

Once you have estimated your income, the next element of your business plan should be an estimate of your expenses. Expenses include the cost of advertising, car and truck expenses such as gas and maintenance, the cost of insurance, office expenses, the cost of

Sample Expense Worksheet

	1	2	3	4	5	6	7	8	9	10	11	12
Advertising Expenses	$ 100	$ 100	$ 100	$ 100	$ 50	$ 50	$ 50	$ 50	$ 0	$ 0	$ 0	$ 0
Automobile Expenses	$ 400	$ 400	$ 400	$ 400	$ 400	$ 400	$ 400	$ 400	$ 400	$ 400	$ 400	$ 400
Insurance	$ 25	$ 25	$ 25	$ 25	$ 25	$ 25	$ 25	$ 25	$ 25	$ 25	$ 25	$ 25
Office expenses	$ 50	$ 50	$ 50	$ 50	$ 50	$ 50	$ 50	$ 50	$ 50	$ 50	$ 50	$ 50
Supplies	$ 25	$ 25	$ 25	$ 25	$ 25	$ 25	$ 25	$ 25	$ 25	$ 25	$ 25	$ 25
Utilities	$ 100	$ 50	$ 50	$ 50	$ 50	$ 50	$ 50	$ 50	$ 50	$ 50	$ 50	$ 50
Company Uniform	$ 25	$ 25	$ 25	$ 25	$ 25	$ 25	$ 25	$ 25	$ 25	$ 25	$ 25	$ 25
Monthly Totals	$ 725	$ 675	$ 675	$ 675	$ 625	$ 625	$ 625	$ 625	$ 575	$ 575	$ 575	$ 575
Total Expenses												$7,550

supplies, and the cost of utilities such as telephone service.

Of all the expenses, the largest continuing expense probably will be travel. For example, I spend over three hundred dollars a month on gas alone. If you are buying a new vehicle, gas mileage is definitely something to consider. The difference between driving a fifteen-miles-per-gallon V-8 truck and a little forty-miles-per-gallon economy car can mean literally thousands of dollars a year. I know this is bad news for you guys out there who like to drive around in big wheels to complement your big muscles; but it is the unfortunate truth.

Use the expense worksheet to estimate your expenses. Divide expenses that you pay out less than once a month into monthly amounts. For example, if you pay for your insurance quarterly, divide the amount of your quarterly premium by three and include it with the other monthly expenses. Total up the expenses in each month's column and put the results in the Monthly Totals row. Then total up the numbers across this row and put the result in the total expenses box. A sample expense worksheet for an imaginary personal training business is provided in the chapter as an example.

3.1.7 Estimating Profits

Once you have filled in the income and expense worksheets, you will be ready to fill in the profit and loss worksheet. The profit and loss work-sheet will tell you what the expected profit or loss from your business will be for each of the first twelve months. Again, a sample profit and loss work-sheet is provided in this chapter as an example.

Fill in the gross income row of the profit and loss worksheet from the gross income row on the income worksheet. Then fill in the expense row of the worksheet from the total expenses per month row of the expense worksheet. Once you have done this, subtract the expenses for each month from the income for each month and put the results in the net income row. Finally, total up the month-by-month figures in the net income row and put the result in the total net income per month row. Note that, by convention, negative values are enclosed in parentheses rather than preceded by a negative sign.

Because initially you will have few clients and little income and as a result of the one-time expenses involved in setting up the business, during the first few months you probably will be running in the red, that is, your monthly net profits will be negative. This should not continue indefinitely. The profits should become positive by the third or fourth month at the very least.

If they do not, you need to rethink your business plan. You either need to increase your monthly gross income by training more clients or charging more money, or you need to reduce your monthly expenses. If necessary, go back to your income and expense worksheets

Sample Profit and Loss Worksheet

Date _____ January 1994

	1	2	3	4	5	6	7	8	9	10	11	12
Total Gross Income per month (from Income Worksheet)	$ 0	$ 960	$ 1,920	$ 2,880	$ 3,840	$ 4,880	$ 5,760	$ 6,720	$ 7,680	$ 7,680	$ 7,680	$ 7,680
Total Expenses per month (from Expense Worksheet)	$ 725	$ 675	$ 675	$ 675	$ 625	$ 625	$ 625	$ 625	$ 575	$ 575	$ 575	$ 575
Net Income per Month	($ 725)	$ 285	$ 1,245	$ 2,205	$ 3,215	$ 4,255	$ 5,135	$ 6,095	$ 7,105	$ 7,105	$ 7,105	$ 7,105
Total Net Income												$50,130

and rework the numbers.

Notice also that by adding up the net income for all the months for which it is negative you will have an estimate of how much money you need to start the business. For example, if you have a loss of $500 the first month, a loss of $350 the second month, a loss of $100 the third month, and positive net income the fourth month, you will know that you need at least $950 to start your business.

Of course, the income and expense worksheets on which the profit and loss worksheet is based are only estimates. As you actually begin your business, you will get a much more accurate idea of what your income and expenses will be. You might find, for example, that you underestimated the cost of operating your automobile. Or, you might discover that clients want to work out fewer times a week than you had expected. Therefore, plan on reworking your income, expense, and profit and loss worksheets periodically to reflect these changes.

If all this sounds somewhat dry and boring, it is. Fortunately, preparing a profit and loss statement does not take long and, once done, is very useful. At the end of each month, by comparing your actual income and expenses to your estimates, you will know exactly how well you are doing. That way, if you are losing money, you will find out before your rent check bounces. And, if you are earning more money than you expected, you will know that you can take the vacation you have been planning or,

better yet, reinvest the money in your business.

3.2 Your Business Name and Logo

One item you need to consider when setting up your business is your business name and logo. Ideally, the name of your business should be somewhat descriptive; it should say what you do. Remember not to make it too specific, though, so as not to limit yourself in the future. If, for example, you start out calling your business Jane's Aerobics and a year down the road decide to branch out into weight training, you are going to have a problem.

Your name and logo also should be catchy, something people will notice and remember. My company, for example, is called Bodies Plus Fitness Systems. It says what I do, but leaves room for me to expand. It sounds professional. And, together with my logo, it looks good on T-shirts and business cards.

Whatever name and logo you choose, once chosen, stick with them. There is no use spending your time and money getting your name known only to change it.

3.3 The Form of Your Business

Another consideration when setting up your business is the form of your business. You can organize your business as a sole proprietorship, a partnership, or a corporation. Each has advantages and disadvantages that you need to consider before making a decision. The following discussion will help you choose the form of business which will best fit your needs.

3.3.1 Sole Proprietorship

A sole proprietorship means that you personally are your own business. This is the simplest form of business to start and run. All income received by the business is considered your income and all expenses are considered your expenses. You can hire employees, but are not yourself an employee.

The advantages of a sole proprietorship are its simplicity. There is no special paper work involved in starting the business. There also is no additional tax return to be filed, only two additional schedules along with your regular individual tax return. You file Schedule C to report your business's income and expenses and file Schedule SE to calculate the Social Security tax on that income.

The disadvantages of a sole proprietorship are that this form of business affords you no liability protection. With a sole proprietorship form of business, you and the business are the same legal and financial entity. As a result, if the business is sued, all of your assets, both personal and business, are potentially liable. In addition, since you are not an employee, you cannot take advantage of certain employee benefits such as group health and life insurance. Finally, there is

no provision for ownership of the business by more than one person.

3.3.2 Partnership

While a sole proprietorship is, as its name suggests, a business comprised of a single person, a partnership is a business comprised of two or more people. A partnership is formed with a partnership agreement. Like the sole proprietor, the partners in a partnership are not employees of the business.

A partnership allows multiple people to own a business while requiring less paperwork than a corporation. It is an easy way for more than one person to create a business and share in its expenses and income.

The major disadvantage of a partnership, as with a sole proprietorship, is that the partners are not shielded from liability, so that their personal assets are subject to the claims of the creditors of the business. The partnership also must file an annual income tax return of its own.

Partnerships have been compared to marriages, and the success rate, 50% or less, is comparable. Careful consideration must be given to the compatibility of the partners before entering into a partnership.

3.3.3 Corporation

Unlike a sole proprietorship or a partnership, a corporation is an entity unto itself. The owners of the corporation, the shareholders, are separate from the corporation. This means that, as owners, they are shielded from personal liability. It also means that they can participate as employees of the business, taking advantage of employee benefits.

The primary disadvantage of a corporation is that it is more complicated to create and maintain. This is a big disadvantage. Large corporations have entire departments which handle the legal and tax paperwork involved in running a corporation. The owner of a small, single-person corporation, however, must do all the paperwork him or herself. This work can occupy a great deal of time which would otherwise be better spent on activities which generate revenue.

> "...you want to spend your time training clients, not holding board meetings and filling out tax forms."

3.3.4 Choosing a Form of Business

A sole proprietorship form of business should be sufficient for almost all but the largest personal training businesses, and I recommend that you organize your business as such. After all, you want to spend your time training clients not holding board meetings and filling out tax forms. You can always incorporate the business later. The discussion in the rest of this chapter on licenses, insurance, bookkeeping, and taxes assumes use of a sole proprietorship, although much of what is said may also be applicable to partnerships and corporations.

If you decide, instead, to set up your business as a corporation, you either can self-incorporate, using one of the many incorporation kits available at bookstores, or have an attorney create a corporation for you. If you choose to do it yourself, it will generally cost under $100. Having an attorney do it for you should cost no more than $500.

As for partnerships, I strongly discourage you from organizing your business in this way. If you are one of several people who want to own a business jointly, you are better off forming a corporation. When you become a general partner in a partnership, you put all of your other assets at the risk of the business. You are not relying simply on yourself, but also on your partners' business acumen and honesty. If you want to form a partnership in spite of this, you should have an attorney draw up a partnership agreement to reduce the risk as much as possible.

3.4 Licenses and Permits

As part of setting up your business you will need to obtain several types of licenses and permits. The exact types you will need will vary from place to place. Below is a description of the most common. While you may avoid obtaining the required licenses and permits without any negative consequences, obtaining them is quick, not very expensive, and will preclude legal problems.

3.4.1 Trade Name Application

You could run your business under your own name. However, because the name of your business is one of the most important types of advertisement you have, you probably will want to use a name which describes the nature of your business. If you use a business name, you will need to file a Trade Name Application. The Trade Name Application, also known as a Fictitious Name Statement, Doing Business As or Assumed Name Certificate, identifies your business name, your real name, your business address, and the nature of your business. The purpose of registering a trade name is to help customers, suppliers, and other interested parties determine the owner of the business with which they are dealing.

Depending on where your business is located, your trade name will need to be registered either with your state government, your local county government, or both. Check with the local county clerk's office for the procedures for filing a Trade Name Application. You can find the telephone number for the clerk's office in your telephone book under the local government listings. As part of your filing, you will be required to pay a fee and may also be required to publish a notice in a local paper.

3.4.2 Business License

In addition to the Trade Name Application, you probably also will need to obtain a business license. As with the Trade Name Application, procedures for obtaining a business license vary from place to place. When you talk to the local county clerk's office, ask about the specific procedures and requirements for obtaining a business license. As with all other licenses and permits, the business license will cost a small fee.

3.4.3 Sales Tax License

Most states do not charge sales tax on services. Check with your state government as to whether or not your state does. If so, you will be required to obtain a Sales Tax License, sometimes known as a Seller's Permit, as well as collect sales tax from your clients and remit the tax to the state.

Even if your state does not charge sales tax on services, if you are planning to sell goods—clothing or fitness equipment, for example—as part of your personal training business, you will need to deal with sales tax. See Chapter VII, *Expanding Your Business*, for more information on obtaining a Sales Tax License.

3.5 Liability Insurance and Client Waiver Form

Liability insurance is one of those items you might be tempted to try to get along without—do not. In a business such as personal training, where clients are involved in physical activity and the possibility of injury is always present, liability insurance is essential. Without it, you could be liable for large amounts of money as a result of a client who rightfully or wrongfully believes you have injured him or her. Without insurance, such a claim could easily ruin you financially, causing you to lose your business, your savings, your investments, your house, and your car. In this litigious society, where people sue first and asked questions later, liability insurance is well worth the money it costs.

Another important reason for obtaining liability insurance is that, sooner or later, you probably will want to work in a gym or health club. Getting into a gym or health club as an independent trainer will dramatically improve your exposure to new clients and provide you and your clients with access to facilities and equipment otherwise unavailable. Before they will even consider allowing you to train clients on their premises, however, a gym or health club will require you to have liability insurance. Generally $100,000 to $150,000 of coverage is sufficient. Before you purchase insurance, check with gyms and health clubs in your area to determine their specific requirements.

In addition to providing proof of liability insurance coverage, many gyms and health clubs will require you to have their name listed as an insured on your insurance policy. This can be done

via your insurance company at any time for a small fee, usually about $25 per name. When shopping for insurance, find out what the insurance company charges for this service.

3.5.1 Obtaining Liability Insurance

The least expensive way to obtain liability coverage is to add it to your renter's or homeowner's insurance policy. This is referred to as a "general liability business pursuits endorsement." When you add this type of liability coverage to your renter's or homeowner's policy, $200,000 of coverage will generally cost less than $100 extra per year. This insurance, however, will only protect you personally; if you have any employees, you will have to find insurance which will cover them as well.

The other option for getting liability insurance is to buy a separate insurance policy. One way to do this is by becoming a member of an organization of fitness professionals such as IDEA and then purchasing insurance through them. All of the organizations listed in Chapter II that provide certification programs for personal trainers also provide liability insurance to members.

When buying insurance through a professional organization, $1,000,000 worth of coverage for your company will generally cost around $500 a year. This policy will cover you and, in some cases, other employees as well. If employees are not covered, they usually can be added to the policy for a small additional charge of typically $10 or $20 per year. While this is a fairly good deal, remember to take into account the cost of membership fees to the organization when calculating the cost of insurance. Membership fees generally will cost from $150 to $200 per year.

3.5.2 Client Waiver Form

In addition to having liability insurance you also should use a client waiver form which all your clients should sign. This waiver form provides added legal protection. On this form, the client acknowledges that the type of aerobic and/or weight training he or she will be engaging in carries certain inherent risks and that, other than for negligence on your part, the client absolves you of any liability for injuries sustained by him or her as a result of the training. A client waiver form is provided in the Forms Section of this book. Whether you use this form or your own, you may want to have it reviewed by an attorney beforehand. Note that a waiver form is not a substitute for liability insurance. I strongly recommend that you both obtain liability insurance and use a waiver form with every client without exception.

3.6 A Business Checking Account

One of the first tasks you will need to perform as part of your new business is to open a business checking account at a local bank. Since this account will be in the name of your business, not your own name, you will need a copy of the Trade Name Application mentioned in Section 3.4.1.

Be aware that business accounts are handled differently from personal accounts. Minimum balance requirements and fees for services are generally higher. Also be aware that there are some services which are generally free for personal accounts—deposits, for example—for which business accounts are charged. To find a bank, call up several in your area. Explain that you are interested in opening a business checking account and ask about the bank's fees and requirements.

When choosing a bank, remember that you want to develop a long-term relationship with the people there. Although at first you probably will be opening a checking account only, you may want later to use the bank for other services such as loans to expand your business or a merchant's account so you can accept payment by credit card. Banks are also a good source of refunds for finding people to provide other business services such as local attorneys and accountants. Therefore, you want to find a bank that caters to small businesses such as yours and has people experience in that area.

The best way to find a bank is by word of mouth. Talk to other small business owners in the area about the banks they use and, perhaps more importantly, the banks they do not use.

Chances are they will be able to steer you in the right direction.

3.7 Bookkeeping

If you thought insurance was boring, bookkeeping will put you to sleep. Like insurance, however, bookkeeping is essential to running a business. And, as with most things, if you organize it well from the start, your bookkeeping system will save you time in the long run. Whatever type of bookkeeping system you use, the single most important point is this: no matter what you do to keep track of money earned and money spent, at least do something. If you neglect bookkeeping, you are guaranteed to have problems.

3.7.1 Choosing a Bookkeeping System

There are two decisions to make when establishing a bookkeeping system for your personal training business. The first is whether to use a single entry or double entry bookkeeping system. In a single entry system, every transaction, whether income or expenditure, is recorded once. In a double entry system, every transaction is recorded twice, as a credit on one ledger and as a debit on a second ledger. The single entry system is simpler to use; the double entry system has a built-in cross check to avoid errors.

Double entry bookkeeping is a business in and of itself. For a simple business such as personal training where

the number of receipts is relatively few and there is no inventory, I recommend using a single entry system. If you want to use a double entry system, you better have experience with bookkeeping or be willing to take an accounting course.

The second decision to be made when setting up your books is whether to use the cash or accrual method of accounting. In the cash method of accounting, income is recorded when received and expenses are recorded when paid. With the accrual method of accounting, income and expenses are recorded when the transaction takes place, when the income is earned, or the expense incurred, regardless of whether or not any money has actually changed hands.

In Chapter IV, *Getting Clients*, I suggest that you have clients pay for several training sessions in advance. Suppose that in January, a client pays you $500 in advance for ten training sessions. During the rest of the month of January you train the client five times. It is not until February that you do the other five training sessions for which the client has paid.

Under the cash method of accounting, income is recorded when you receive it. Therefore, in the previous example, you would record the entire $500 of income for January, the month in which you received it. None of the income would be recorded for February. Under the accrual method of accounting, however, income is recorded when earned. Therefore, in the same situation, you would record only $250 of income for the month of January. The remaining $250 would be recorded for the month of February.

A similar situation occurs with expenses. Suppose that you pay quarterly liability insurance premiums of $150 due in advance the first of January, April, July, and October. Under the cash method of accounting, expenses are recorded when paid. Therefore, in this example, you would record an insurance expense of $150 for the months of January, April, July, and October. No insurance expense would be recorded for the other months of the year.

Under the accrual method of accounting, however, expenses are recorded when incurred. Therefore, in this same example, an insurance expense of $50 would be recorded for each month of the year. The expense of insurance is incurred equally during each month of the year, not just during those months you pay the insurance premium.

I recommend using the accrual method of accounting. It may take a little more work than the cash method. But as you can see from the preceding examples, it will provide you with a much better idea of how much money you are actually earning and spending. Income and expense ledgers suitable for a simple personal training business are provided in the Forms Section of this book. The instructions in this chapter for using these ledgers assume single entry accrual accounting.

If you do not want to use the ledgers provided, but want to set up your own ledgers instead, you either can buy entire bound ledgers or separate sheets of ledger paper with binder holes. Ledgers and ledger paper are available with different numbers of columns. For your income ledger you probably will need no more than four columns. For your expenditure ledger, however, you may need as many as ten. Ledger books and paper are available from stationary and business supply stores.

3.7.2 *Invoices*

In Chapter IV, *Getting Clients*, I describe how and when to charge clients. I suggest that clients should be required to buy a group of at least three and preferably ten training sessions at a time. These sessions should be paid for in advance. When the last of these sessions is up, the client should buy another group of sessions. This system reduces the amount of paperwork which would be required if the client paid for each session individually. It also reduces the possibility that you will have to chase after a client for your fee.

Whenever a client buys a group of training sessions—or anything else—from you, you should provide him or her with an invoice. The form of the invoice is very straightforward. Your company name, address, and telephone number should appear at the top. This should be followed by the date and a unique invoice number. This, in turn, should be followed by the client's name and address. The body of the invoice should list the number of training sessions the client is buying, the fee per training session, the sales tax if any, and the total amount due. An invoice for personal training services is provided in the Forms Section of this book.

When you create an invoice for a client, always create a duplicate for yourself. Clients normally will pay you at the time you give them the invoice. Occasionally, however, a client may not be able to pay you immediately. Any invoices which have not been paid should be kept separate from those that have. When the client eventually pays, you should take the unpaid invoice, mark it as paid, and file it with the paid invoices.

> "...for accrual accounting, always record income regardless of whether or not you have actually been paid."

3.7.3 Posting Income

While your invoices will provide you with a record of money received, they will not, with the exception of merchandise, provide you with a record of income earned. That is because the client will be paying for training sessions in advance. The income will not be earned until you actually perform the training.

Your record of earned income is your appointment book. In your appointment book, you should maintain a careful, day-by-day record of who you trained and when. Since you also will be maintaining a list of scheduled clients in your appointment book, you need to

carefully distinguish between clients who you were scheduled to train and clients who you actually trained. Inevitably, a client who you were scheduled to train will cancel at the last minute and a client who you were not scheduled to train will ask to be squeezed in.

Periodically—preferably at the end of every day on which you trained clients and at least once every several days—you should post income to your income ledger. The income ledger contains one row for every day of the month. Using your appointment book, add up the total income for the day you are posting income and record it on the appropriate line. Non-taxable sales—such as income from personal training in states where services are not taxed—should be recorded in the non-taxable sales column. Taxable sales should be recorded in the taxable sales and the sales tax columns. List the total sale minus sales tax in the non-taxable sales column and sales tax in the sales tax column. In addition, always fill in the total column with the total income which should be the sum of the previous three columns. Remember, for accrual accounting, always record income regardless of whether or not you have actually been paid.

3.7.4 Posting Expenditures

Just as you should post all income to

the income ledger, you should post all expenditures to the expenditure ledger. Whenever you spend money, you should record the expenditure in your expenditure ledger. This should be done at the time you incur the expense, even if you have not yet actually made payment.

Each expenditure should be recorded on a separate line. You should record the date, the payee, and the amount. When you actually pay the amount, you also should record the number of the check used to pay the expense. You should avoid paying expenses in cash if at all possible; paying by check provides you with a paper trail. If you do pay an expense in cash, write the word "cash" in the check number column instead.

Use separate columns in the ledger to distinguish between different types of expenditures. There are two reasons for categorizing expenses. The first and most important reason is for tax purposes. In order to claim tax deductions, the IRS requires that you divide expenses into certain categories. The expense ledger provided in this book contains the categories you probably will need to run a small personal training business. For more information on the categories of expenses you need to maintain for tax purposes, get IRS Publications 535, *Business Expenses*, and 334, *Tax Guide for Small Business*. A form for ordering these and other IRS publications is provided in the Forms Section of this book.

The second reason for dividing expenses into categories is to provide you with information for managing your business. You want to maintain categories which will be useful for preparing financial statements, such as the expense worksheets provided in the Forms Section. As with the income ledger, regardless of which column you list an expense in, list the expense in the total column as well.

3.7.5 Totalling up the Ledgers

No matter how often you post income and expenditures, make sure that you total your ledgers at the end of every month and at the end of every year. At the end of every month, add up each of the columns and put the total of each column in a separate total row at the bottom of the ledger. Then sum the totals of all the columns except the total column. This sum should match the figure in the total column. If it does not, you have an error somewhere. Recheck your arithmetic.

Similarly, at the end of every year, add up the monthly total rows for every month and put the totals in a yearly total row. Then sum all the totals of all the columns except the total column. Again, this sum should match the figure in the total column.

3.7.6 Bad Debts

You will note that in the accrual accounting system, unreceived income is recorded on the income ledger. At the end of the year, gather your unpaid invoices and total up your unpaid accounts. If you never expect to receive this income, it is considered as uncollectible and a business expense that you can take as a tax deduction.

3.7.7 Getting an Accountant

The personal training business is not a complicated one from a bookkeeping standpoint; income and expenses are fairly straight forward, and there is no inventory. You should not, therefore, need an accountant for your day-to-day bookkeeping or taxes. You may, however, want to meet with an accountant once or twice when you are first starting your business to help you set up your bookkeeping system. Not only will he or she be able to get you off on the right foot, you also will have someone to call when you have questions or problems.

3.7.8 Bookkeeping with a Personal Computer

By now, I suspect, your eyes are probably about to glaze over. You may very well be thinking that making money will not be much fun if you have to spend so much time and energy keeping track of it. I warned you that running a business would be a lot of work.

Fortunately, accounting software is available for personal computers that can do a lot of the bookkeeping work for you. With the software, you simply enter income and expenses into the computer as they occur. The computer performs all the calculations. Invoices, income and expense reports, profit and loss statements, and numerous other reports can be generated quickly and easily. Many programs will keep track of bank accounts and even print checks.

If you have a personal computer or are thinking of getting one, I strongly recommend that you consider purchasing accounting software. An accounting program can relieve a small business owner such as yourself of a lot of the drudgery and opportunity for error involved in bookkeeping with pen and ledger. It also will free up your time for doing more important things such as training clients. For more information, see the discussion later in this chapter on purchasing computer hardware and software.

3.8 Taxes

It was Mark Twain who said that nothing in life is certain except death and taxes. You probably already believe in the certainty of death. If, however, you have any lingering doubts about taxes, you will become a believer once you start your own business. Calculating and paying taxes are important parts of any small business; you need to be familiar with tax requirements and procedures.

The following discussion is not intended to be a thorough or complete description of everything you need to know about taxes. Rather, it is intended to alert you to principal areas you should know about regarding taxes and your personal training business. For more information, get IRS Publication 334, *Tax Guide for Small Business* and consult an accountant.

3.8.1 Deductible Expenses

In business, it is not how much money you earn, but how much you keep that counts. With current tax rates, you will be paying approximately a third of your taxable income to the government. The key phrase here is *taxable income.* That is, your gross income minus deductions. For businesses, deductions include virtually all business expenses. The more expenses you can deduct, the less your taxable income, and the less tax you have to pay on the same amount of gross income. Therefore, one of the most important aspects of your business will be keeping track of deductible expenses. This will be almost as important as actually earning money.

In the personal training business, one of the biggest deductible expenses is the cost of operating your car or truck. As I said before, gas alone will cost several thousand dollars a year. Add to this maintenance and repair costs and you have a significant amount of money.

There are two ways to deduct automobile expenses: by the actual expenses incurred or by taking a mileage allowance. Get IRS Publication 917, *Business Use of Car,* for instructions on deducting automobile expenses. It is a good idea to get this publication *before* you start your business. It explains which expenses you need to keep track of during the year in order to substantiate a deduction. If you wait until tax time to obtain this information, it will be too late.

Other likely deductible expenses you may incur in your personal training business include: advertising expenses; the cost of insurance; office expenses; the cost of supplies; and the cost of utilities such as telephone service. Get IRS Publication 535, *Business Expenses,* for a complete discussion of the expenses you are allowed to deduct and how to deduct them. As with the instructions for deducting automobile expenses, get the publication *before* you start your business to ensure that you understand how to keep track of expenses during the year in order to claim a deduction at tax time.

3.8.2 Quarterly Estimated Tax

If you have ever worked as an employee, you certainly are familiar with federal and state income tax withholding. When you were hired, you filled out a W-4 form on which you specified how many exemptions you were claiming and thus how much tax would be withheld from your paycheck. Then, each time you were paid, the company you worked for withheld a certain percentage of your pay. This money, essentially an advance on your income tax, was sent to the government. At tax time, you compared the amount withheld during the year with the amount of tax owed. If the amount withheld was less than the tax owed, you owed the government additional money and reluctantly included a check with your tax return. If the amount withheld exceeded the tax owed, the government owed *you* money and you anxiously awaited a refund.

As a self-employed person, there is no one to withhold income for you. Therefore, if you will owe more than $500 in taxes, you will need to pay quarterly estimated tax during the year. This estimated tax takes the place of the withholding from a paycheck. If you do not pay quarterly estimated tax, you will owe additional interest and penalties at tax time. Get IRS Publication 505, *Tax Withholding and Estimated Tax* and Form 1040-ES, *Estimated Tax for Individuals*, for more information. The instructions with Form 1040-ES tell you how to determine whether you need to pay estimated tax.

Estimated federal tax is due quarterly on April 15, June 15, September 15, and January 15. Estimated state tax is usually due on the same dates, but may differ slightly in some states. Check with your state department of taxation for instructions on calculating and paying estimated state tax.

Just as you should not let an employer withhold more of your pay than necessary, you should not overpay estimated tax. Although you will receive a refund at the end of the year if you do overpay, you will be lending the government the excess money without receiving interest. Despite popular excitement

over tax refunds, as long as you are careful not to accrue any interest charges or penalties, you are actually better off owing the government money at tax time than receiving a refund.

Note that, if you are starting your personal training business part-time while working for someone else, you may want to avoid paying estimated tax by increasing the withholding from the income from your other job. To do this, first calculate the tax you will owe from both your other job and your personal training business. The instructions provided with IRS Form 1040-ES, *Estimated Tax for Individuals*, can help you do this calculation. Then, from your pay stubs, determine how much has been withheld so far and project how much will be withheld over the balance of the year. Subtract the total amount withheld already and the amount to be withheld from the estimated tax due. If the result is that you will owe more than $500 to the IRS, divide the extra tax due by the number of pay checks you have left for the year. Have your employer withhold the additional tax by filling out a new W-4 form.

Also be aware of the "safe harbors" provision of the tax code. Normally, the amount of estimated tax paid or salary withheld must equal at least 90% of the amount of the tax you owe. The "safe harbors" provision allows you to underpay estimated tax and withholding as long as the amount of estimated tax paid or salary withheld is greater than or equal to the total amount of tax you owed the previous year. This only works when your income one year is greater than your income the previous year. It means that you can delay paying a larger portion of the tax you owe until tax time. Remember, however, that you are simply delaying payment. When you file your yearly tax return on April 15th, you will owe the remainder of the tax. For more information on "safe harbors," get IRS Publication 505, *Tax Withholding and Estimated Tax* and Form 1040-ES, *Estimated Tax for Individuals*.

3.8.3 *Your Tax Return*

At tax time, in addition to Form 1040, you also will need to fill out Schedule C, *Profit or Loss From Business*, and Schedule SE, *Self-Employment Tax*. Both these schedules are easy to complete, provided you have been keeping good records during the year. Instructions for filling them out are included in the 1040 instruction book. Note that if you have not been self-employed before or have had considerable unearned income, these schedules probably will not be included in the copy of the 1040 booklet that the IRS automatically sends you. If that is the case, you can obtain the necessary forms at your local Post Office, library, or by writing to the IRS.

In addition to federal taxes, you may owe state and possibly local taxes as well. Fortunately, these taxes are small compared to federal taxes and require considerably less paperwork. Check with the department of taxation in your state for procedures on calculating and paying state and local taxes.

While on the subject of taxes, let me say something about cheating. If you have been working for someone else and most of your income has been coming from your salary, you have had no opportunity to cheat on your taxes. Every cent that you are paid is recorded on a W-2 form that is supplied to the IRS by your employer.

When running your personal training business, this will change. You will receive a lot of money for which there will be no record, particularly if you are paid in cash. You may be tempted not to report some of this money and cheat on your taxes. Do not even think of doing this. The IRS is one of the scariest organizations in the federal government; they seize property first and ask questions later. If caught cheating on your taxes, you will be in serious trouble. More importantly, though, by cheating on your taxes you will not only be cheating the IRS, you will be cheating the rest of us who do pay our fair share.

3.8.4 *Taxes with a Personal Computer*

As with accounting, tax preparation can be done by hand. However, also like accounting, tax software which will prepare taxes for you is available for personal computers. With this software, you enter information such as income and deductible expenses and the computer does the necessary tax calculations. If you have a laser printer, the computer will generate completed tax forms as well.

It is also possible to obtain accounting software and tax software that work together. With this arrangement, the tax software automatically picks up the necessary information, such as income and deductible expenses, directly from the accounting software. This feature eliminates the need to enter your financial information twice.

Tax software not only saves you time; it removes most opportunities for errors during tax preparation. Even if you do not want to trust your taxes to a computer, you may want to use a tax program to check your own manual tax calculations. If you are interested in purchasing tax software, see the discussion later in this chapter on purchasing computer software and hardware.

3.9 Telephone number

When starting your personal training business, you probably will be working out of your home. One dilemma you may encounter when setting up a home-based business is whether to get residential or business telephone service. In general, telephone companies frown upon the use of residential telephone service for business purposes. This is because the telephone company charges more for business service than for residential service. If you plan to have two different lines, one for personal use and one for business use, you should select business telephone service for the line you are using for business use. If, however, you plan to use the same line for both personal and business calls, then it probably is better to select residential service. In this latter case, you can easily justify selecting residential service on the grounds that the telephone's primary use is for personal calls.

Although business telephone service is more expensive than residential service, there are some advantages to it. One advantage of having a business telephone line is that it allows you to place a listing in the Yellow Pages directory. In my experience, however, people do not shop for personal trainers in the Yellow Pages, making a Yellow Pages listing a benefit of little value to you. Another advantage of having business service is that it give you the ability to choose your telephone number. This can be useful in any business, including personal training.

An alternative or addition to business telephone service is to get a toll-free (800) number. A toll-free number can be set up either with its own telephone line, or with an existing telephone line. For example, I have a single business line which is also a toll-free line. My local business number and my toll-free number use the same line.

You can get a local toll-free number, which can be used only within your state, or a national toll-free number. Unless you also are involved in a business such as mail-order or are located near a state line, a local toll-free number is probably sufficient.

Toll-free service is not much more expensive than business telephone service. The cost generally includes a hookup fee, a flat monthly charge (usually $20 to $40 per month), and a per-minute charge (usually 15 to 30 cents per minute) which depends on the time of day of the call.

National toll-free service is offered by the various long distance telephone companies, AT&T, MCI, and Sprint. Due to competition, companies often run specials that waive the hookup charge and include some free call time. Local toll-free service is offered by your local telephone company. If you decide to get a national toll-free number, shop around.

If you get business telephone service or a toll-free number, choose a number, if possible, which people can easily remember. Some examples of local numbers for a personal training business are 555-FITT, 555-TRIM, 555-THIN, 555-PUMP, 555-DOIT. Obviously you would substitute your local exchange for 555. Toll-free numbers give you more flexibility when selecting a number. As with your company name and logo, once you choose a telephone number, stick with it.

3.10 An Answering Machine

Since, at least in the beginning, you will be spending most of your time at the houses of clients, in gyms and health clubs, or on the road, you will need an answering machine to take calls when you are not around. This is essential for

---

List of Toll Free Number Companies

The following companies offer national and international toll free 800 number service:

AT&T
(800) 222-0400

MCI
(800) 888-0800

Sprint
(800) 877-4646

---

allowing new clients to get in touch with you as well as for allowing existing clients to make schedule changes.

There are many different brands of answering machines, varying in features and price. The cheapest ones use a single cassette tape. This tape is used to record not only messages left by callers, but also your outgoing message that is played whenever someone calls. More expensive machines use dual tapes, one for incoming messages and one for the outgoing message. Finally, the most expensive machines use no tapes. Instead, they record incoming and outgoing messages digitally on a computer chip similar to the memory in a microcomputer.

I recommend avoiding single tape machines. They tend to be slower and less reliable than the more expensive ones. Either choose a dual tape or digital machine. I have a dual tape machine which I like very much. I also know people who have digital machines and rave about them.

Whatever model you choose, the

major criterion for selecting a machine should be the total available recording time. In the personal training business, you can expect a lot of calls while you are out. You need a machine that will not run out of recording space. The one drawback of digital machines currently is that they tend to have relatively short total recording times. The technology is advancing rapidly, however, so this will not be a problem for long.

Another essential feature to look for when choosing an answering machine is remote access. Since you will be on the road a lot, you want to be able to call up your answering machine from a remote telephone and retrieve messages. All but the most basic answering machines sold today allow you to do this.

A slightly more professional alternative to an answering machine is voice mail. Most telephone companies offer this service for a monthly fee of $10 to $20. The Bell Atlantic telephone company refers to this service as "Answer Call." Voice mail is also available from other companies. If you are interested in voice mail, check with your local telephone company and look in the Yellow Pages under TELEPHONE for additional voice mail companies.

The most professional, but also most expensive, alternative to an answering machine is to hire an answering service. With a service, your calls will be answered by an operator. This is probably an unnecessary expense for a small personal training business. But, if you are interested in getting an answering service, look in the Yellow Pages under TELEPHONE for answering service companies.

3.11 A Pager

Regardless of the type of telephone and answering system you have, you probably also will want a pager. A pager will enable clients to get in touch with you to make last minute changes. For example, although I stress to clients that cancellations should be made twenty-four hours in advance, frequently a client will page me a few hours or even a few minutes before a session to cancel or reschedule. Without the pager I would have to check my answering machine constantly.

Pagers either can be purchased or leased. Pager companies often will sell you a pager cheaply, sometimes even give one to you for free, to encourage you to use their service. The cost varies depending on the type of service you want. The most basic service generally costs between $10 and $20 a month.

3.12 Why You Do Not Need A Cellular Phone

It might seem at first glance to make more sense to forget the answering machine and pager and just get a cellular phone. It would be very convenient and you might be tempted to do just that. Cellular phones, however, can become very expensive very fast. The basic service is typically $50 to $75 per month; and that is the cost before you make any calls. Unlike standard telephone service where you pay only for calls you make, with cellular phone service, you pay both for calls you make and for calls you receive—anywhere from 25 to 50 cents a minute. If you make a long distance call, there will also be a long distance charge.

At least when starting your business, it probably is best to avoid cellular phones. A pager along with an answering machine, voice mail, or answering service should satisfy your needs. If and when you decide to purchase a cellular phone, exercising some restraint in using it by keeping conversations short and avoiding unnecessary calls is essential if you want to avoid huge telephone bills.

3.13 Business Cards and Brochures

Business cards are essential for your personal training business. You will meet potential clients in all sorts of places: while working out in the gym, shopping at the supermarket, or mailing a letter at the Post Office. You should carry business cards with you wherever you go so you have them ready to give to people at all times.

One of the best sources of new clients is referrals from existing clients. If you can do it gracefully, give some of your business cards to your existing clients and ask them to pass them on to their friends and relatives.

Your business card should include your company's name, your company's logo, your name, your title, and telephone numbers. Even if you are working by yourself, including the company information and giving yourself a title will lend more credibility to you and your organization even if you are your company's only employee. Also, make sure that the business card clearly indicates the nature of your business.

A business card does not have to be fancy, but it should be professional. However, if you have a great physique and are willing to spend some extra money, you can put a photograph of yourself on the back of your business card, which is a common practice among personal trainers. If you use that type of advertisement, be sure the card presents the image you want to project to attract the types of clients you are trying to acquire. The purpose of business cards, after all, is not to boost your ego, but to get new clients.

In addition to business cards, you also should have brochures that describe you and your company. Brochures will provide everyone, from potential clients to newspaper journalists who write stories about you, with information about you, your company, and the services your company offers.

Brochures should include the company name and logo, a list of employee credentials, a list of any professionals such as physicians or chiropractors associated with your company, and a description of the services you provide. Do not include any prices on your brochure.

Check with local printers about having business cards and brochures printed or look under PRINTERS in the Yellow Pages.

3.14 A Company Uniform

Although I have mentioned it already, it bears repeating that you and your employees are by far the most important form of advertising you have. One way to take advantage of this is to have a uniform, a company shirt and shorts for example, created specifically for you and your employees. This will help ensure that you and your staff always look neat and professional as well as alert potential customers to your business. A uniform is particularly useful if you are training clients in public places such as gyms and health clubs where you will be seen by lots of other people interested in physical fitness.

The least expensive type of uniform is a T-shirt with your company name and logo. Alternatively, you can have short sleeve knit shirts embroidered with your name and logo on the breast pocket. This will be more expensive than T-shirts, but also will be slightly more professional looking. I do both. I have knit shirts that my staff and I wear and T-shirts that I give to my clients.

Look in the Yellow Pages under T-SHIRT for companies that do silkscreen printing on T-shirts and under UNI-FORMS for companies that embroider logos on knit shirts and other apparel.

Mail order companies such as Land's End also do embroidery. The clothing from them is usually of better quality than that from uniform companies—with 100% cotton rather than synthetic fabrics, for example—but is also more expensive.

If you decide to have clothing designed for you, whatever you do, do not put your telephone number or address on it. Remember, you want to look like a fitness professional, not the local Maytag repairman.

3.15 Why You Need a Personal Computer

Strictly speaking, a personal computer is not essential equipment for a personal training business. In fact, you can get along very nicely without one, as I did until quite recently. However, personal computers are becoming increasingly more important to running a successful small business. I could not, therefore, finish this chapter without at least mentioning them.

3.15.1 Why Buy a Personal Computer

A personal computer can simplify many of the tasks involved in running a personal training business. I have already mentioned the benefits of using a computer for accounting and tax purposes. Although these are probably the two most important areas where a personal computer would be useful in your personal training business, there also are other tasks which a computer could simplify.

A personal computer is useful for desktop publishing and graphic design. As part of your personal training business you will want to create marketing materials such as flyers. While you could have these designed by a local print shop or graphic artist, desktop publishing and graphic design software would allow you to do this yourself. This is not only faster and cheaper than having someone else do it, it is a lot more fun. In fact, you might even decide to produce a regular newsletter on your computer to keep your clients and potential clients informed about the services you offer.

A computer also is useful for maintaining databases and mailing lists. Keeping track of current and former clients is an important part of any personal training business. Database software would allow you to track a variety of client information, from addresses and telephone numbers to medical and training data. You could then generate mailing lists to specific types of clients. For example, you might start a program geared to senior citizens and only want to send flyers to your clients over age sixty-five. You also could create graphs of training data to give to clients documenting their progress over time.

A computer also is useful for developing financial statements. Using a program called a spreadsheet, income statements, expense statements, and profit and loss statements can be generated and modified quickly and easily. Change one number in the statement, and all the other numbers based on that number are automatically recalculated. If you have ever tried to prepare these types of statements by hand with pen, paper, and calculator, you have an idea of how much time a computer can save.

Finally, a computer is probably most useful for word processing. This book, for example, was written using a personal computer. Without the computer, the task of writing the book would have been much more difficult—if not almost impossible. Even if you are not writing a book, however, there will be lots of other things you will need to write in the course of running your business.

3.10.2 *How to Buy a Personal Computer*

Once the decision to buy a personal is made, many people rush out to the nearest computer store and purchase the first computer they see. This is not the way to go about buying a computer. Buying a computer should be a rational, logical process.

Before shopping for a computer, the first step is to determine the principal uses of the computer. You may have in mind several major as well as some minor uses for the computer. The major uses should be the driving force underlying your choice of computer. You need to choose a computer which is well-suited to handle these major tasks. The minor uses should not motivate your choice of computer; however, be sure that whatever computer you purchase, it can handle these secondary tasks. For example, you might want a computer primarily for word processing and accounting. However, you also might want to use the computer for accessing computer bulletin boards and networks.

The second step to buying a computer—once you have determined what your primary and secondary uses for it are—is to select appropriate software programs for each of these uses. In most cases, there will be several different software programs that serve the same purpose and you will need to choose among them. The best way to decide on the appropriate software is to talk to people who are already using it. For example, if you want to use your computer for wordprocessing, find people who already are using computers for wordprocessing and talk to them. Find out which software programs they are using and what hardware—the computer equipment—they are running the software on.

Computer magazines are another good source of information on software. Your local library should have a good collection. Look through recent issues for articles on the types of software programs you are considering to buy. Remember, however, that the computer industry is changing very quickly and that magazines older than a year are probably of little use.

Once you have chosen the software programs you will be using, the third step is to decide the type of hardware to buy. Most software has minimum system requirements that tell you what the minimum hardware required to run the program is. As you are investigating software programs and talking to people who are using them, keep track of the types of hardware on which the software is being run. Frequently, the minimum system requirements are insufficient to actually run the software successfully and efficiently. People who already are using the software should have a better idea of exactly what you need.

Hardware requirements include the type and speed of the microprocessor, the amount of memory, the amount of disk space, and the type of display. The display consists of the computer monitor and the associated video board which is located in the computer and to which the monitor attaches. Once you have bought a system, increasing the amount of memory and disk space is relatively easy while changing the microprocessor and the display is not. Therefore, if you want to skimp on something initially to save a little money with the idea of improving the system later, it is generally better to skimp on buying memory and disk space than on the type of microprocessor or display. Buy the most powerful microprocessor and highest resolution display you can afford.

The fourth and final step in buying a computer is deciding from whom to buy it. Armed with your list of software and hardware requirements, you should be ready to talk to computer vendors. Call up some of the major mail order computer companies and give them your list of requirements. A list of some of the larger mail-order computer vendors is provided in this chapter. Also, check with local computer stores. Shop not only price, but service as well. Pay attention to warranties and return policies.

List of Mail Order Computer Vendors

The following are some of the largest and most reputable companies selling personal computers and personal computer software by mail:

ALR (Advanced Logic Research)
(800) 444-4ALR

Compaq
(800) 345-1518

Dell
(800) 283-0088

Gateway 2000
(800) 846-2065

IBM
(800) 426-2968

NCR
(800) 627-8315

Zeos
(800) 554-5220

Chapter Four
Getting Clients

The key to running a successful personal training business is getting and retaining clients. If you do not have any clients, you do not have a personal training business, no matter what it says on your business card. This chapter describes the three most effective techniques that I know for getting new clients as well as what to do once you have gotten them. Take advantage of the free time you have now, when you are first starting out, to follow the steps described below. Then take a look at Chapter V, *Getting into Gyms and Health Clubs*, and Chapter VI, *Advertising and Publicity*, for some additional ideas on generating new business.

4.1 Getting Referrals from Physicians

Over the years I have tried many techniques for getting new clients; some have been successful, many have not. Of all the techniques that I have tried, by far the most effective has been getting referrals from physicians and other health care professionals. You may not be aware of this, but physicians and health care workers, such as chiropractors, regularly refer patients to personal trainers. As people generally trust physicians, potential clients are more likely to try your services if referred to you by their physician than if they read an advertisement for you in a newspaper or see your flyer on a bulletin board.

You might think there is not much you can do to generate referrals from physicians and that you just have to wait for one to mention your name. This is not true. You can and should actively work to encourage local physicians and health care workers in your area to refer clients to you. Doing so is easier than you might think.

You probably have at least one physician yourself; if you do not, you should. Start by approaching him or her. If it is time for your annual physical or you have another reason for seeing the physician, you can use this as an occasion to bring up the subject. If not, schedule an appointment specifically to discuss it.

When you meet, explain that you are a personal trainer, and provide the physician with a copy of your brochure.

Make sure that he or she is aware of any credentials and experience you may have. If you already have clients who are patients of the physician, make sure he or she knows this as well.

Once you have told the physician who you are, explain what you can do for his or her patients. This will depend on the types of services you offer and the types of patients the physician sees. Typically, the most important reason physicians will want to refer patients to you is weight loss. You might, for example, talk to a gynecologist who has a female patient who needs to lose some weight after a pregnancy. Or, you might meet an internist who has a male patient who needs to start exercising because of high blood pressure.

Keep in mind, however, that although weight loss will be the primary reason most physicians will refer patients to you, there will be others as well. A physician in geriatrics, for example, might want to refer an elderly patient to you for strength training. Similarly a psychiatrist might be interested in the benefits of regular training sessions for a patient with depression. When talking to the physician, make sure that he or she is aware of these additional benefits that training with you can offer.

Cardiologists, if you know one, are particularly valuable sources of referrals. A good way to approach a cardiologist is to tell the physician that you require all new clients who are over forty or who have potential heart problems to undergo a stress test before you begin

working out together, and that you are looking for a physician to whom you can send clients in order to have this done. Suggest to the physician that he or she refer patients to you, and you refer clients back to him or her.

Once you have exhausted your own physicians, try your friends' and relatives' physicians. Orthopedists also are good sources of referrals. Who do you know who has seen an orthopedist recently?

No matter what type of physician you are talking to, remember that they are highly educated, intelligent, motivated people who frequently have very little patience and even less time. This often makes them intimidating. The best way to deal with them is to know what you want to say ahead of time, be clear and specific, and keep your conversation as brief as possible. Be sure of yourself and what you have to say, but leave any arrogance at the door. Most importantly, once you have finished talking, keep quiet, listen carefully, and be prepared for hard questions and possible objections.

Besides discussing referrals, you also may want to offer the physician some free training sessions. Not only will training the physician enable you to demonstrate the types of benefits you can offer his or her patients, but in addition, since physicians usually have the money to invest in a personal trainer, they are themselves potential clients. Even if the physician does not refer anyone else to you, he or she may become a permanent client, and having a physician as a client always adds to your credibility.

Before you leave the physician's office, no matter how well or badly the conversation went, be sure to ask if you can put some of your business cards, brochures, or flyers in the waiting room. That way, even if the physician does not refer anyone to you, patients will see your literature and may take the initiative to call you themselves or at least ask the physician about you. See Chapter VI, *Advertising and Publicity*, for tips on creating effective brochures and flyers.

It should take you a week at most of telephoning and leg-work to become associated with at least one physician in your area. If you are having trouble, be persistent. Having a relationship with a physician is an important source of clients; it will be well worth the effort.

4.2 Getting Referrals from Equipment Stores

Another excellent way to get new clients, besides referrals from physicians, is through referrals from fitness equipment stores. These are stores that sell exercise and fitness equipment such as weight machines, exercise bikes, and treadmills. As part of your personal training business, you should develop a relationship with at least one of these types of stores.

Start by locating likely stores in your area; you probably already know of some. If not, check the Yellow Pages and

your local papers. Avoid large chains since they have corporate policies and red tape which make it difficult for a small business such as yours to deal with them. Your best chance is with independent stores and small chains. If there is a store in your area that sells equipment only, try it first.

Once you have identified a possible store, set up a meeting with the owner or manager. Explain who you are and provide him or her with a copy of your brochure. Make sure the owner is aware of any credentials and experience you may have. If you have any newspaper or magazine articles written about you, provide a copy of these as well; store owners always appreciate good publicity.

Offer to let the store include a free consultation with you whenever a customer buys a certain dollar amount worth of exercise equipment. The owner should jump at this opportunity; it provides the store with something extra to entice customers to buy their equipment while not costing them anything.

You will provide the store with brochures and flyers describing your company and services. The store should give these to customers who are considering purchasing certain types of equipment. They can tell the customer that if he or she buys the equipment, the store will provide a personal trainer to come to the customer's home and explain how to use it. Once a customer has bought a piece of equipment, the store should contact you with the customer's name and telephone number. You will then contact the customer and arrange for the free consultation.

While this process is simple, there are several important details that should not be overlooked. First, the store should offer your services only with the purchase of certain types of equipment. You and the store need to decide in advance what types of equipment this will be. Remember, you only want to give free consultations to customers who buy expensive pieces of equipment, not just any piece of equipment the store sells. The purpose is to generate useful leads that provide you with new clients, not waste your time with lots of training sessions for which you will not get paid.

Second, the store should not set up the consultation sessions itself; you should. This gives you total control of when and where you do the sessions. You particularly want to avoid giving free consultations in the store itself. Setting up the consultation sessions yourself also ensures that you get the names and phone numbers of the customers so you can add them to your mailing list.

Third, the store should not wait for a customer to buy a piece of equipment to give him or her your brochure. The store should give your brochure to any customer who even considers buying a piece of equipment which qualifies for the service. That way, even if the customer leaves without buying anything, he or she will have your brochure and may decide to call you anyway.

And finally, make sure that the agreement between you and the store —which, of course, should be in writing—can be terminated by you at any time. When you are first starting out, you may think that having too many clients is like being too rich or too thin—that there is no such thing. Your business will reach a point, however, when you do not need or want any more clients. When that happens, as unlikely as it may seem, any free consultation you have to do, even if it leads to a new client, is a waste of your time. Therefore, when you set up the arrangement with the store, make sure you can stop providing free consultations as soon as it is no longer beneficial for you to keep doing them.

Later in this chapter, I describe in detail how to perform a standard free consultation. The free consultation you give customers who have bought equipment will be the same as the one you give all potential clients, except that it will include showing the customer how to use the equipment he or she has just purchased. In spite of this difference, however, the purpose will be the same: to get the customer to hire you on a permanent basis.

Having followed all the steps outlined above, you may find that, even so, the store owner is not interested in participating with you in this arrangement. If this is the case, do not become discouraged; there may be other ways that you and the store can work together. Chapter VI, *Advertising and Publicity*, describes how to work with a store on promotional ideas such as coupons and gift certificates. You may want to discuss some of these with the store owner. In any case, before you leave the store, be sure to ask if you can leave some of your business cards, brochures, or flyers for customers to pick up. If you get nothing else from the store, at least you may be able to leave some of your literature where customers will see it.

4.3 Generating Business with Free Programs

Besides referrals from physicians and fitness equipment stores, another excellent way to find prospective clients is to provide free programs for local organizations. Offer to give a free lecture on a health or fitness-related topic for the local Rotary or Cranes club, for example. These types of organizations are always looking for people to speak on interesting subjects. Giving a free program for them will provide you with free advertising and an opportunity to meet people in the area who might be interested in your services.

If you offer this type of free program, make sure you get as much publicity out of it as possible. Prepare flyers describing the program you are offering as well as who you and your company are. Have the organization post these flyers and, if possible, mail them to their members. Remember, the purpose of providing a free program is to find paying clients. So, make sure the flyers

contain enough information about you and your company so that people reading them can contact you directly if they are interested in one-on-one personal training.

Another way to get involved in free programs is to allow your services to be auctioned at a charity auction. To do this, contact the local chapters of national nonprofit organizations such as the National Kidney Foundation. Black tie auctions are best since they attract upper middle class and wealthy people who can most afford your services.

Offer to allow the organization to auction three or four free training sessions with you. The organization running the auction will prepare a pamphlet for those attending which describes each item being auctioned. If possible, prepare the description of your services yourself. Again, make sure that it contains enough information about you and your company so that people reading it can contact you directly. Although only one person at the auction will get your services, everyone will be reading the description, and a losing bidder or even someone who did not bid, may be interested in hiring you.

The advantage of using charity auctions to find prospective clients is that whoever ends up getting your services has to pay a lot of money for them, much more than you would usually charge for a couple of sessions. This probably means that the bidder is seriously interested in using a personal trainer. Otherwise, he or she would have bid instead on a year's supply of Chateaubriand or a weekend getaway on Nantucket. Because of this, whomever you end up training could very likely become a permanent client.

Even if you decide not to offer any other type of free program, I highly recommend having your services auctioned at least once. You have very little to lose and everything to gain by doing so. I have given my services to charity auctions several times; every time, I have gotten at least one permanent client as a result.

Whatever free programs you decide to do—if any—keep this in mind. Be careful not to overextend yourself. Although free programs are an excellent way to meet potential clients, you are not getting paid for them, and your time is money. When you are first starting out and have a lot of time on your hands, you probably can afford to do a free program once a week. As you become busier, though, you will want to limit yourself to once a month or less.

4.4 Your First Conversation with a Client

If you follow the techniques described above for generating client leads, sooner or later a prospective client is going to call. This is your initial contact with the client so it is vital that you make a good first impression.

I have found, for some strange reason, that new clients almost always call at the worst possible times. My breakfast is burning, I just cut myself shaving, I am late for an appointment, the phone rings, and it's a new client. Remember, when this happens, you must sound professional, no matter what else is going on. If you cannot manage this, ask the client if you can return his or her call, deal with the emergency, and call the client back as soon as possible. This is far better than sounding rushed or, worse, incompetent.

When talking to the client, it is important to realize that the goal of this first phone conversation is not to sell your services; all you want to do at this time is to qualify the client—make sure the client is serious—and then get into his or her house for a free consultation. Just as a door-to-door salesman might put his foot in the door to prevent the owner of the house from closing it before he or she has had time to make a sales pitch, so you will use the free consultation as an uninterrupted opportunity to sell the client on hiring you. The initial phone conversation is simply a time for you to arrange to give the potential client a free consultation—to get your foot in the door.

This being the case, during the first phone conversation the client probably will do most of the talking. That is okay. It will make the client feel comfortable, and there is not much you need to say at this point anyway.

Just make sure that before the conversation ends you set up an appointment with the client for a free consultation. To do this, explain to the client that you do not train anyone without first doing one free consultation session. The consultation session is a time for the two of you to get to know each other, for you to explain your services, and for the client to explain his or her goals. It is also a time for you to evaluate the client's current health and fitness. Since the consultation session is free, if the client has any real interest in training with you, you should have very little trouble getting him or her to agree to it.

As you are talking to the client during this first phone conversation, whatever else you say, as a general rule you should not mention price. Your services are expensive; you want to make sure that you have a chance to sell the client on the benefits of hiring you before you discuss how much it is going to cost. Otherwise, you may scare the client away and never get the chance to sell your services. Of course, if the client asks you directly how much you charge, you will have to say; you do not want to seem evasive. But, do not bring up the subject if the client does not mention it.

The only exception to this rule is if you want to qualify the client. For example, if the client is some distance away or you have some doubts about the person's intentions, you may want to make sure that he or she is genuinely serious about hiring a personal trainer. Mentioning your price is one way to do this. In the beginning, however, even this is probably not a good idea; when you have few or no clients, you do not want to cut off potential leads too early.

4.5 The Free Consultation

Once you have found a potential client, the job of getting the client is only half over. You must now convince the person to hire you. You also must make sure that the individual is someone you want to train—someone, for example, who can pay for your services and who is in good health. As I said before, to accomplish these things you should provide all prospective clients with a free consultation before you begin training with them.

The free consultation should be conducted in person wherever the two of you will be training. This usually will be the client's home or a local gym or health club. The consultation session should last anywhere from a half hour to an hour. You need enough time to evaluate the client and sell him or her on hiring you, but you do not want the session to drag on too long; after all, you are not getting paid for it.

When you go to this initial meeting with the client, be conscious of the importance of first impressions. If you are training the client at home, you will be coming into this person's house regularly. Although you need to convince the client that you are knowledgeable about exercise and fitness, just as important, you need to make the client feel comfortable with you. Making the client feel comfortable and at ease has as much to do with how you look and act as with anything you say, so dress and act accordingly.

4.5.1 *The Consultation Plan*

When you first meet, after small talk about the weather or the difficulty you had finding the house, you should start off the consultation session by briefly telling the client about yourself. You will want to mention your education and certification. If you have clippings of newspaper or magazine articles about yourself, you might give copies of these to the client as well. And, if you are training someone the client might know, a local physician for example, you should mention this as well. Regardless of what you say, be brief; do not bore the client.

Once you have told the client about yourself, you need to find out what the client hopes to gain from a regular fitness program. Clients' interests can vary greatly, and it is important that you evaluate their goals and expectations. Questions to ask include: "Why did you call?", "Where do you hope to be in three months?", "In six months?", etc.

Once you have an idea of the client's expectations, it is time to evaluate the client's health and physical condition. Things to consider are flexibility, strength, any injuries or conditions that have to be taken into account when exercising, and, most important, any physical condition that would make it dangerous for the client to exercise. The physical evaluation is one of the most important parts of the free consultation, so take your time. Clients initially may be reluctant to discuss health problems

---

Consultation Check List

- ☐ Give the client a copy of your brochure
- ☐ Briefly tell the client about yourself
- ☐ Ask the client what he or she is looking for in a fitness program
- ☐ Listen carefully to the client
- ☐ Evaluate the client's health and physical condition
- ☐ Remind the client that you are not a physician
- ☐ If client has medical problems or is over forty, request that he or she see a physician before you begin training
- ☐ If you do not wish to train the client, tell the client
- ☐ Give the client a realistic assessment of what the two of you can accomplish
- ☐ Close the sale by asking the client when he or she wants to start
- ☐ Discuss what you charge and acceptable forms of payment
- ☐ Discuss the minimum number of training sessions the client is required to agree to
- ☐ Have the client pay for the first set of training sessions
- ☐ Give the client an invoice for the first set of training sessions
- ☐ Have the client sign the Client Waiver form

---

with you; you need to encourage them do so. A sample health questionnaire is provided to assist you.

As you listen to the client and evaluate his or her condition, it is very important that you remind the client that you are neither a physician nor qualified to make a medical diagnosis. If the client has any medical problems or has not seen a physician recently, have him or her provide you with a letter from a physician before you begin training. Requiring the client do this is for your protection as much as for his or hers.

> "Do not focus on how much the client will have to pay.... emphasize the benefits which the client will receive for his or her investment."

Regardless of health, any client over forty should undergo a stress test before beginning to train. You can ensure that the client does this by explaining that your insurance company requires it. As I mentioned earlier, it is a good idea to have an arrangement with a cardiologist to whom you can refer clients for this purpose.

Once you have evaluated the client's goals and physical condition, it is time to give the client a realistic assessment of what the two of you can accomplish. If the client's goals are realistic, that is great; you are all set. If not, you need to indicate this to the client—gently but clearly. Be diplomatic, but do not make promises you cannot keep; they will come back to haunt you. In addition, if the client's expectations or physical condition are such that you do not wish to train him or her, now is the time to say so.

At this point in the consultation, if everything else has gone well, the client should, with any luck, be ready to start training with you. Now is the time to close the sale. This is done by asking a question that forces the client to make a commitment, such as when do you want to start or when should we plan to have our first training session? Note that, whatever you say, you should phrase it with the assumption that the client has decided to hire you. Avoid questions, such as do you want to train with me or are you interested in hiring me? Such questions give the client the opportunity to turn you down. There are many books devoted entirely to the subject of closing a sale; if you are interested, check your local library and bookstores.

You also might want to visit some car dealerships. Car salesmen are masters of high pressure sales tactics. While I do not recommend all of their methods, you can learn some valuable sales techniques—how to close a sale, for example—by watching them in action.

If the client has not brought up the subject of price already, closing the sale by asking for a commitment will almost certainly cause him or her to mention it. You need to discuss the price now. Hopefully, you have been successful in selling your services, so the client already has decided to train with you, and price is not a problem. If it is, you need to strengthen your sales pitch. Do not focus on how much the client will have to pay; the truth is that you are expensive. Instead, emphasize the benefits which the client will receive for his or her investment.

4.5.2 *What to Charge*

One of the most difficult decisions you have to make before you find your first client is how much to charge. Charge too much and you risk losing potential clients; charge too little and you may earn less than you otherwise might earn. As an added complication, once you start training a client at a certain rate, it is difficult, if not impossible, to raise your rate. I have this problem. My newer clients all pay seventy dollars an hour. I have older clients, however, who are still paying forty. While I might be able to raise the rates of my forty-dollar-per-hour clients $5 or $10 per hour per year, if I increased the rate any more than that, I would lose them.

The best way to determine your rate is to investigate other trainers and personal training companies in the area and find out what they charge. Some people suggest that if you are new to the business, you may want to undercut the competition's price slightly for the first few clients. I already have discussed the dangers of competing on price. When I first started, the competition was charging sixty dollars an hour, so I decided to charge thirty. In retrospect, this approach did not generate many additional clients while it cost me income I otherwise would have earned.

If you do decide to offer a discount, wait to do so until you have a sense of how much the client is willing to spend. Keeping in mind that it is hard to raise your price once a client has been training with you for awhile, let the client know that you are offering a special discount for a specific number of initial sessions only. That way, when the time comes, it will be a lot easier to raise your rate.

Also, when you do finally tell the client what your rate is, be aware that some clients like to haggle. You will quote them a price and although they probably think it is reasonable and they can easily afford it, they will insist on negotiating a lower rate. They just need to have the satisfaction of getting a bargain. It is very strange to be sitting in a million dollar house with a man whose personal net worth exceeds that of some small countries and have to argue with him over five or ten dollars an hour. It happens, however, more often than you would imagine.

If you sense that you are in this type of a situation, do yourself a favor; quote a price ten or fifteen dollars higher than you expect to get. When the client starts haggling, do not give in immediately, but hold firm at your original price. Then, after you have told the client why you cannot possibly charge any less and resisted for a reasonable amount of time, reluctantly give in to the lower price.

The net result is that the client is happy because he or she got a great deal and you are happy because you are being paid what you expected to be paid.

4.5.3 *The Number of Training Sessions*

Besides price, you also need to negotiate with the client the number of training sessions he or she initially will purchase. You want to get a commitment from the client for several sessions up front. The reason for this is that it takes a few sessions for the client to become accustomed to working out and for you to be certain that the client understands the exercises.

With a client who intends to train with you at least once per week, try to get a commitment for ten sessions. If the client is unwilling to commit to ten sessions or intends to train with you infrequently—once or twice a month, for example—obtain a commitment for at least three sessions. If a client is not willing to commit to even this small number of sessions, he or she probably is not serious about training with you, and you are wasting your time.

Since my business is located in the Washington, D.C. area, I am fortunate enough to have a large pool of potential clients who are willing and able to afford my services on a weekly basis. Therefore, I have geared my business toward clients who are interested in

> "In many regions of the country...it may be necessary to rely more heavily on clients who want to use a personal trainer on a less frequent basis."

working out at least once per week; in fact, most of my clients train with me even more frequently. In many regions of the country, however, where there are smaller concentrations of people able to afford the services of a personal trainer every week, it may be necessary to rely more heavily on clients who want to use a personal trainer on a less frequent basis.

Clearly, the client who trains with you once per month is less lucrative for your business than one who trains with you once per week. Just because a client trains with you infrequently, however, does not mean that he or she is not a good client. A client who trains with you consistently every couple of weeks—or even once a month—could be a valuable client.

It is possible to build a personal training business with clients who train with you regularly, but infrequently. Keep in mind that it requires a much larger client base, so plan accordingly. A larger client base means additional work on your part both to find clients and to keep track of them. If you are not located in or near one of the major cities in the country, however, you may have no choice but to organize your business to accommodate clients who only can afford to train less than once a week.

While you may want to consider clients who intend to train with you infrequently, avoid clients who intend to train with you only once. Every so often you will come across someone who wants to hire you for only a single session. Perhaps the client cannot afford you on a regular basis or perhaps he or she does not understand that obtaining results takes time. Whatever the reason, he or she insists on a single session. It may be tempting, especially when you are just starting out, to accept the offer. You may figure that, after all, some work is better than none—especially when the rent is due.

As a rule, I advise against this. Every client involves a certain amount of overhead regardless of how many times you train. You have to fit the client into your schedule, evaluate the client's health and fitness, and collect payment from the client. This overhead is acceptable if you are training the client multiple times. It becomes less so if you are training the client only once.

If you do decide to train a client for a single session—and even I occasionally may—you should do so for a good reason. For example, you might decide to do a single session if the client is a friend of one of your permanent clients from whom the training session is a gift. Never take on business out of desperation, however, just because you think that you will not get any permanent clients. You need to be patient and have faith that you will find people who will want to hire you on a permanent basis. If you do not believe this, then you should find another line of work, because that is what running your own

personal training business is all about.

4.5.4 *The Method of Payment and Cancellation Policy*

Payment for your services should always be in advance; never train anyone on credit. That way, you are guaranteed that the client is serious about training with you for at least the number of sessions for which you have been paid. It also saves you the trouble of collecting money from clients at every session or, worse, chasing after clients who owe you money.

During the free consultation, have the client pay for the initial group of sessions agreed upon. Then, when the client gets to the last prepaid session, have him or her pay for another group of sessions. For example, if the client agrees to ten sessions, have him or her pay for the ten during the free consultation. Then, at the tenth session, have the client pay for another ten.

The one exception to this rule which you may want to make is for clients who you train infrequently. If I am training a client once a month, for example, after the initial group of sessions, I usually will allow the client to pay on a session by session basis. When I let a client do this, however, I make certain that he or she pays me at the time of each session.

Once you have decided on how much the client is going to pay and for how many sessions, you need to decide on the method of payment. Payment usually should be by check. This creates a paper trail in case there is a disagreement over if and when the client paid. It also forces you to deposit the money. Accepting cash may be tempting but dangerous; the opportunity to lose track of your income is too great. As your business grows, however, you may want to consider accepting payment by credit card. See Chapter VII, *Expanding Your Business*, for information on handling credit cards. Whatever you decide to do, let the client know the forms of payment that you accept at the time of the free consultation.

Along with determining a method of payment, you need to establish a policy on cancellations. My policy, for example, is that clients must pay for any session that is not canceled at least twelve hours in advance. I cannot tell you how many times I have arrived at a client's house only to have the client appear at the door and tell me that he or she cannot exercise today. This takes up my time, and I expect to be reimbursed for it. What is more, since I carry a pager, there is no excuse for it.

Once you have developed a policy on cancellations, whatever it is, make sure that your clients are aware of it and adhere to it. The best idea is to give the policy to your clients in writing. That way, there is no doubt that you informed them of your cancellation policy.

Similarly, if *you* cancel at the last minute or arrive extremely late, give the client a free session. Doing so will compensate in good will for what you lose in income. Of course, never cancel

the first session with a client; that is not the way to begin your relationship.

4.5.5 *The Client Waiver Form*

Before you leave the free consultation or, at the very latest, at the beginning of the first training session, you need to ask the client to sign a waiver form. The best time to do this is after you have closed the sale and while the client is writing out a check. Whenever you approach the subject, however, do not spook the client by mentioning the waiver form until you have closed the sale. The client waiver form is described in more detail in Chapter III, *Setting up Your Business*.

Chapter Five
Getting into Gyms and Health Clubs

While you probably will start your business by training clients in private homes, eventually you will want to become associated with a gym or health club as an outside trainer. Most gyms and health clubs maintain a better selection of equipment than even the best-equipped home gym. Training your clients at a gym will enable you to provide them with much more varied and interesting workouts than otherwise possible. This will help your clients remain motivated from session to session and, in turn, help ensure that they continue to train with you.

In addition, working in a gym or health club also will provide you with added exposure. While training your clients, you will be surrounded by other members, all of whom have at least some interest in exercising and staying in shape. Some members may want to hire you. Working as an outside trainer in a gym or health club can be a valuable source of new clients.

Finally, affiliation with a gym or health club is another item to add to your list of credentials. Although getting into a club as an outside trainer is often

simply a matter of having the right insurance, potential clients will see your relationship with the club as proof that you are a *bona fide* personal trainer. As a result, to be able to say that you are associated with one or more gyms or health clubs in the area can be very useful in convincing potential clients to hire you.

5.1 How to Get into a Gym with a Member

The easiest way to get into a gym or health club as an outside trainer is to find a new client who is not already a member but wants to become one. While most new clients will hire you specifically to work out at home, some may want to join a club. Even if a client comes to you with the intention of working out at home, however, he or she still may be agreeable to joining a gym or health club if you can suggest a suitable place nearby. The best type of client for this would be one who does not already have a lot of equipment and would find joining a club easier and cheaper than setting up a home gym.

Explain to the client the benefits of working out in a gym or health club, but do not force him or her to join. Remember, the most important aspect of your job is to make sure that the client feels comfortable; if he or she prefers to work out at home, then so be it. The two of you can always switch your workouts to a gym or health club later.

If you have a client who wants to become a member of a gym or health club—one with which you are not yet associated—have him or her contact the club first. The client should tell the club that he or she is interested in joining but would like to bring in an outside personal trainer. Warn your client that the club probably will offer the services of an in-house trainer instead, and that he or she should decline this offer. The client should agree to become a member only if the club allows you to come in as an outside trainer.

Gyms and health clubs do not make money when people *use* them; they make money when people *join* them. Getting new members is the bread and butter of their business. If bringing you in as an outside trainer will help the club get a member, most clubs will let you in. If not, there probably are other gyms and health clubs in the area; have your client look elsewhere.

5.1.1 Getting an Existing Client to Become a Member

If you cannot find a new client who wants to join a gym or health club, you might convince an existing client to do so. Perhaps you have a client who has been working out with you for awhile in the home. He or she may have some basic equipment or you may bring dumbbells and other equipment along with you each time you come. As you work out together and the client progresses, he or she gradually will need heavier weights and more equipment. Eventually, he or she may advance to the point where it would be more convenient for the two of you to train at a local gym or health club rather than at home. This is a perfect opportunity for you to get into a gym or health club as an outside trainer.

5.1.2 Getting a Member to Become a Client

If you do not have any new or existing clients who want to become members of a gym or health club, another option is to try the opposite approach: to find someone who is already a member of a gym or health club who wants to become a client. Start by identifying one or more local gyms or health clubs in the area that offer the best chance of finding a client. Generally, the more expensive the club, the more luck you will have finding a member who wants—and just as important, can afford—a personal trainer.

Once you have identified a likely place, ask the club if you can post your flyers on the premises. Since you are not already associated with the gym or health club, the management may not look kindly on this; they either may stop you before you put up your flyers or tear them down after you leave. If you run into this problem, do not despair; there always are alternatives. Try stopping by the gym or health club during peak hours—weekday evenings or Saturday afternoons, for example—and put your flyers on cars in the parking lot. Chapter VI, *Advertising and Publicity*, discusses how to create and distribute flyers.

5.2 How to Get into a Gym Without a Member

If you do not have either a client who is or wants to become a member of a club or, a member of a club who wants to become a client, you are in a difficult situation. The only way to become associated with the gym or health club may be to approach the club cold—that is, without a member. While this is not as easy to do as when you already have a client who wants to train at the club, it is possible.

Talk to the gym manager or, in a large facility or chain, the fitness director. Call first to set up a meeting. Remember that gym managers and fitness directors are busy people who talk to would-be personal trainers every day. Do not be discouraged if your first call is not returned. Be persistent without being annoying or rude.

When you meet with the gym manager, be ready to provide proof of

insurance and a description of what services you want to offer in the gym or health club. Make sure the gym manager is aware of any credentials and experience you have; you need to convince him or her that you are a competent personal trainer. Most importantly, stress the benefits of having an outside trainer such as yourself in the club. You will advertise the club in your flyers and other literature. You will bring new members into the club. And, you have knowledge and skills that the in-house staff do not.

As an added incentive to the club, offer to do some free seminars for them. Particularly good topics for health clubs with a lot of women are programs on abdominals; hips and thighs; and nutrition. The club usually will help you advertise your seminars by photocopying your flyers, posting signs, and listing the seminars in club calendars and literature. Although you are offering the seminars for free, they are worth your time and effort; giving them encourages the gym or health club to allow you to train clients in their facility and provides you with free advertising and the opportunity to meet potential clients.

5.3 Gym and Health Club Requirements

When you become an outside trainer, be aware that the gym or health club usually will want a percentage of the income from clients you train in their facility. This amount will vary depending on whether your client is a member of the club. Some clubs allow outside trainers to train nonmembers in the club. If your client is not a member, the percentage will be higher than if your client is a member.

If you are self-insured, the club should take no more than 25% of the fee you charge the client, regardless of whether the client is a member. If the club insists on a higher percentage, find another place to train your clients. However, in the unlikely event that the club is insuring you (and if you are not an employee of the club, this scenario is not likely to occur), fifty percent is not unusual. This is yet another reason it pays to have your own insurance.

Some clubs charge a monthly fee instead of taking a percentage. This fee usually depends on the number of clients you train in the club and can be as little as $30 per month per client. Regardless of how the fee is calculated, you should pay no more than 25% of your income from the clients you train in the club. If it costs you more than that, you need to raise the rate you are charging your clients, increase the number of sessions per month you train in the gym, or find another place to train your clients. Generally, if you are doing a lot of training in a club, a fixed fee is less expensive and therefore preferable to a percentage. Usually, however, you will not have a choice; you will have to accept whichever method the club uses to calculate the fee.

Besides a percentage or monthly fee,

be aware that a gym or health club also will require you to have liability insurance before it will let you train clients on its premises. If you checked with gyms and health clubs in your area for the amount of coverage they require before you purchased insurance, as I suggested you do in Chapter III, you should not have any problem meeting this requirement.

As proof of insurance, you will need to provide a copy of your insurance certificate endorsed to include the club as an insured. Adding a club to your insurance certificate can be done for a small fee of approximately $25 by contacting your insurance company. See Chapter III, *Setting up Your Business*, for a discussion of obtaining insurance and adding names to your insurance certificate.

5.4 Gym and Health Club Etiquette

One advantage of being associated with a gym or health club as an outside trainer is that, besides training clients there, most clubs will allow you to use their facilities yourself when you are not working. Although there may be restrictions on when and how you can use the club, such as only on off-peak times or only on weekday mornings, this is a valuable perk that can save you the expense of joining a gym or health club yourself. Remember, however, when you are in the gym or health club, even working out by yourself, you are on stage. Be careful of what you say and do; this is no time for stupid remarks or silly behavior. Clients or potential clients will be watching you, and as a personal trainer, your reputation is vital to your success.

Also, be careful not to alienate in-house trainers and other staff. As you probably are aware, in-house trainers and staff in gyms and health clubs are generally not very well paid. While you may make upward of fifty dollars an hour, the in-house trainers are probably making no more than ten. They know this and you know this. The disparity in income alone will generate some jealousy and animosity. Treating the in-house staff with respect and avoiding anything that could be interpreted as elitism is the best way to avoid problems and maintain a healthy work environment for everyone.

Chapter Six
Advertising and Publicity

In Chapter IV, *Getting Clients*, I described three ways for finding clients which I consider most effective. If you are looking for ways to acquire new clients and have not yet tried the techniques in that chapter, I suggest you do so. This chapter describes additional ways of generating new business through free publicity and paid advertising.

6.1 Word of Mouth

When you start thinking of ways to publicize your business, you may initially think of sending out mailings and other types of paid advertisements. These are excellent ways of generating interest in your business. Before you spend a penny, however, you should consider the various type of free publicity available to you.

The most important form of free publicity for your business is word of mouth. In fact, word of mouth is probably the single most important way for a personal trainer to find new clients. That is why in Chapter IV, *Getting Clients*, two of the three methods I suggest you start with, getting referrals from physi-

cians and offering free programs, both involve building a solid reputation.

Many of my clients have come to me by way of referrals from other clients and acquaintances. In fact, I have one client who, over the years, has referred to me fifteen additional clients. That kind of publicity is better than any advertisement I could have bought at any price. When thinking about publicizing your business, do not forget about your current clients and other people you know; they are the most valuable type of publicity you have.

6.2 Generating Publicity with a News Release

The local news media is another important free publicity resource of which you should take advantage. The basic tool for using the news media to generate publicity is the news release. The news release is the modern form of press release; it includes radio and television in addition to the press.

Whenever your company undertakes something new or noteworthy—when you initially start your business, when you introduce a new product or service, when you become associated with a new gym or health club, when you acquire an important new group contract—send a news release to local newspapers, television, and radio stations. It does not matter how small the news is; the important thing is to get you news into print. Media organizations will not always have room for your news. On a given day, however, they may be eager for additional material.

6.2.1 Form of a News Release

News releases should be printed on your letterhead. At the top of the news release the words "News Release" should appear. Beneath this, the name and telephone number of someone the editor can contact for more information should appear. In a large organization, this would be the name and phone number of a marketing representative. In your case, this should be your name and business telephone number.

As with a news story, a news release should start with an interesting headline which will attract the reader's interest. The text of the news release should read like a news story. In fact, many publications will want to use it almost word for word. Do not start off talking about your business. The first paragraph should be a description of the problem or opportunity that your business is going to address. For example, suppose you are writing a news release announcing new, low impact step aerobics classes. You probably would want to spend the first

---

News Release Check List

☐ Print the news release on your letterhead

☐ Put the words "News Release" at the top of the page

☐ Include the date which the information should be released or the words "For immediate release..."

☐ Include the name and phone number of someone an editor or reporter can contact for more information

☐ Start the body of the news release with an attention-getting headline

☐ Describe an interesting problem or opportunity which your business intends to address

☐ Describe your product or service and how it will address this problem or opportunity

☐ Describe yourself and your company

☐ Include your company's phone number so that customers can contact you

☐ Mail the news release to a specific person in a 9 x 12 inch envelope, hand addressing it if possible

---

paragraph discussing regular high-impact aerobics classes and the problems and disadvantages associated with such high-impact sports.

Once you have described the problem you are addressing, then you can mention your business. In the second paragraph you should describe the services you are offering and how these services address the problem you have

Sample News Release

Bigtown Personal Trainers
100 Main Street, Bigtown, USA
(555) 555-5555

NEWS RELEASE

For immediate release...

Contact: John Smith
(555) 555-5555

Help for the Fitness Dropout

Exercise is good for you. By now, even the die-hard couch potato realizes this even if he is loath to admit it. But knowing what's good for you and going out and doing something about it are two different things. Staying motivated to workout day-to-day, week-to-week is difficult, especially for busy professionals. It was bad enough when the health community recommended aerobic exercise to strengthen our heart and lungs, and we had to get on our treadmills or stairclimbers for twenty minutes. But now we are told that, in addition to aerobics, we should be doing weight bearing exercise to strengthen our muscles and bones.

Fortunately, there is help. John Smith announces the opening of Bigtown Personal Trainers, a one-on-one personal training company. Bigtown Personal Trainers will provide your own private personal trainer who will train you in your home or at a local gym or health club. Whether you're looking to lose weight, tone and trim, or get bigger and stronger, Bigtown Personal Trainers can help you attain your goals. Not only will your trainer keep you motivated; he or she will also ensure that your workouts are as effective and safe as possible. That means you will see more results and fewer injuries. Best of all, personal trainers from Bigtown Personal Trainers are easily affordable. In fact, given the importance of good health, you probably cannot afford to be without one.

John Smith has a B.S. in sports medicine and is certified by the American College of Sports Medicine as are all the trainers who work for his company. For more information call (555) 555-5555. The first consultation with a trainer is FREE, so you have nothing to lose by calling. Call now. Remember summer is not that far away.

#

defined. Again, for example, if you plan to announce the introduction of step aerobics classes, you would describe the classes you are offering and how these classes address the problems encountered with the high-impact aerobics you mentioned earlier.

The last paragraph of the news release should be an overview of you and your business. Describe who you and your business are and what services and products you offer. Be sure to include the name of your company and your telephone number. You want your company name and telephone number in the news story so that interested people can reach you.

The language of the news release should, like a news story, be concise and easy to read. If at all possible, keep it to one page; a news release is more likely to be read if it is brief. I suggest that you follow the three paragraph format I detailed above: one paragraph to describe a problem or opportunity; one paragraph to describe how the product or service you are offering addresses this problem or takes advantage of this opportunity; and a final paragraph to describe you and your business. If you are unable to describe your business and the services you offer in three, brief paragraphs, you probably need to sit down and develop a clearer idea of what you want to say.

Finally, when writing the news release, keep in mind your goal: to increase your business. You are not writing the news release to build your

ego or see your name in print. Stress the benefits, not the features. In other words, do not try to convince the reader how wonderful you and your business are. Try to convince the reader how much better off he or she will be after using your services. A sample news release for the launching of a personal training business is included in this chapter.

6.2.2 News Release Mailing List

Developing a news release is not enough; you have to get it to the local news media and into print or on the air. You could address a news release simply to an organization. You can increase the chance that your news release will be used, however, by addressing it to the specific person who handles fitness and health related news.

Before you send out your first news release, call up local newspapers, radio, and television stations. Find out the name, mailing address, and—if possible—telephone number of the person who handles fitness and health stories. You then can address the news release to that specific person. If you are unable to get the name of a specific person, at least address the release to a specific department. Over time, you will build up a mailing list of contacts in the news media to whom you send news releases.

6.2.3 Mailing the News Release

Each news release should be mailed in a large 9 x 12 inch envelope. Your news release will get more attention this way than if it is folded and mailed in a standard business size envelope. As I said above, if at all possible, the news release should be addressed to a specific person. To help ensure that it gets opened, consider addressing the envelope by hand—if you have the time and the penmanship skills. People are more likely to open a hand addressed letter because it does not look like a mass mailing.

Once you have completed the news release package, take it to the Post Office and find out the amount of postage required. With this information, you can buy the necessary postage for all of the envelopes you plan to mail for the new release.

You probably will want to send your press releases by first-class mail. This will get them to their destinations in several days and will cost you 75 cents or less each, depending upon their weight.

If you want your news releases distributed more quickly and do not mind spending more money, you could send them by Priority Mail. This will get them to their destinations in two days or less. However, sending your news releases by Priority Mail will cost you $2.90 per item.

If you do decide to send your news releases by Priority Mail, go to the Post Office and pick up some Priority Mail envelopes—the hard cardboard ones not the soft floppy ones. The post office provides these envelopes free of charge.

Also purchase the necessary Priority Mail stamps. Since Priority Mail postage is $2.90 for any package not heavier than two pounds, you should not have to worry about weight.

Sending your news releases in Priority Mail envelopes with their red and blue Priority Mail logo not only ensures that they will get to their destination in two days or less. Since Priority Mail is used for important mail, it also ensures that your news release will be opened.

6.2.3 *Following Up on the News Release*

Once your news releases are sent out, you may think that your job is over; it is not. In fact, your job may have just begun. When you compiled your mailing list, you recorded not only the address of each contact, but also his or her telephone number. Once you have sent out your news releases, you need to follow up with the people to whom you sent them. Wait a week or so and then call up each person. Find out if he or she plans to use the information you sent and, if so, when. If the person is not going to use your news release, find out why. Perhaps he or she needs some additional information. Or perhaps a photograph would be helpful. Be polite but persistent. You may need to call back several times.

You want to establish a friendly, ongoing relationship with the people handling fitness and health stories in the local news media. When one of your contacts receives a news release from you, you want him or her to be eager to open it to find out what new and interesting information you have sent. When one of your contacts runs your news release, make sure you send him or her a thank you note. Better yet, if you have some company T-shirts or other apparel, send one of those as well. While this will not guarantee anything, it will help ensure that next time you send a news release, your contact will at least remember your name.

6.3 Offering Yourself as An Expert

Another way to take advantage of the local news media is to offer your services as an expert in health and fitness. Newspapers, magazines, television, and radio stations regularly do stories on fitness and health related topics. As part of these stories, reporters need to obtain the opinions of experts in the field; you are one of those experts.

Take advantage of this. Write a letter offering your services as a health and fitness expert and send it to your contacts in the local news media. To establish your credentials, include with the letter a copy of your brochure and reprints of any articles about you or your company. The next time a story on a health or fitness related topic is being conceived, the reporter may call on you for your insight. A sample letter to a newspaper is included in this chapter.

6.4 Creating Your Own News Story

A news release will, at best, generate a small news item. A better, but also much more difficult, way to use the local news media is to create an entire news story of your own. To do this, you need to come up with a catchy idea for a story which highlights you and your business. Human-interest type stories are always a good choice. If you have any unique clients—ones who are using your services in interesting ways—you might consider creating a story around them.

Suppose, for example, that you are training a son, father, and grandfather in the same family. That is an interesting idea. It appeals to different age groups. It has a family-oriented angle. And it would provide opportunities for interesting photos. The story could be entitled *"Trainer Trains Three Generations of a Family"* or something to that effect. Of course, it is not the opening of Al Capone's vault or the discovery of who shot President Kennedy. But remember, this story is intended for the local news media, not "60 Minutes."

Once you have a good idea, call your media contacts. If you are a reasonably good writer, a local newspaper might want you to write the story yourself. Otherwise, a reporter will do the writing.

When meeting with the reporter, be prepared with your brochure and flyers. If other news sources have written stories about you and your company,

MAXIMIZE YOUR FITNESS

POTENTIAL

With

BODIES   PLUS

Fitness Systems

- Decrease fat
- Increase strength
- Slow down aging process
- Improve cardiovascular condition
- Enhance sports game
- Rejuvenate your workout

Our experienced/certified instructors will work with you, one-on-one by appointment, to give you the individual attention you deserve.

Available in the home, office, or gym.

Individual or Group
Call now to schedule a FREE Fitness Consultation.

(301) 963-FITT

Now there are NO EXCUSES.

provide copies of those as well.

Remember that reporters are always under deadline. They will appreciate any written information about you and your company you can furnish them. As with news releases, this provides you with an opportunity to help determine what information is printed about you and your company; so take advantage of this.

If the story involves personal training, in addition to written material, have at least one client for the reporter to contact. Make sure that this client is someone who will say good things about you and your business. Also, be sure that he or she is reasonably attractive in case the publication wants to take pictures.

I have said it before, but it bears repeating: when dealing with the media, be sure you thank reporters whenever they write something favorable about you. Actively develop relationships with reporters and next time you have an idea for a story, you will find them much more receptive.

6.5 Advertising with Flyers

In Chapter IV and the first part of this chapter, I gave you a half-dozen very effective free publicity techniques. If you are content to build your business slowly and want to avoid spending unnecessary money for advertisements and publicity, you may not need or want to do any paid advertising. If, on the other hand, you want to take a more agressive approach to getting clients, the

rest of this chapter describes how to throw some money at the problem without just throwing money away.

One of the least expensive methods to advertise is the creation and distribution of flyers. Flyers are generally single-page advertisements whose purpose is to entice a potential client to call you. Of all the paid advertising techniques that I have tried, flyers are the ones that I have used the most regularly and with the best results.

6.5.1 Layout of a Flyer

The first component of a flyer should be an attention-getter. The purpose of the attention-getter is to grab people's attention and entice them to read the flyer. An attention-getter can be text or an illustration or both. A good example is my elephant flyer, a sample of which is included in this chapter. This flyer starts with the headline, "How do you look from behind?" Beneath this is a line drawing of the rear end of an elephant. This has been my most successful flyer. Women, in particular, are concerned about excess weight around the hips. This flyer catches their attention.

After the attention-getter should be a list of the services you offer. Keep this brief and easy to read. Remember, the purpose of the flyer is not to convince the client to hire you; it is simply to entice the client to call. Of course you should include your name and phone number. You also should include any credentials, awards, and areas of special

How do you look from behind?

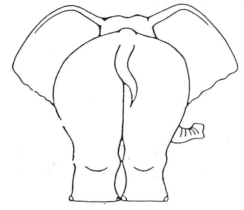

BODIES *Fitness Systems* **PLUS**

Personal Training

•

Insured-Certified Male/Female Instructors

•

"5 Years of Fitness Success Stories"

•

Train with the Best . . . Forget to Rest!

•

301-963-FITT

Owned & Operated by Marla Footer, RN & Ed Gaut, Exercise Magazine for Men's Mr. Exercise.
Also, awarded "Top 10 Most Fit Man in World" at Mr. Fitness Worlds, 92.

ization.

In Chapter IV, *Getting Clients*, I discussed the role of the free consultation. Make sure you include an offer for a free consultation on the flyer. If you want, you even can include a coupon for the consultation. Of course you always offer a free consultation to prospective clients anyway. But the person reading the flyer does not know this. The word "free" is known in advertising to catch attention; use it to your advantage.

Finally, whatever you put on the flyer, do not include your price. As I have said before, your services are expensive. You do not want to scare away potential clients before you have a chance to talk with them. Also, your price may vary depending on who your client is and where he or she wants to work out. For these reasons, listing your price would be a mistake.

6.5.2 Distributing Flyers

Once you have developed a flyer, you need to distribute it.

The cheapest way to distribute flyers is by hand. Flyers can be placed on cars in the parking lots of local gyms and health clubs. With the owner's permission, flyers also can be placed at stores. Good types of stores for your flyers are cleaners, video stores, health food stores, and diet centers.

Another more expensive way to distribute flyers is by mail. This costs more money than distributing flyers in parking lots, but this method also is more effective.

To obtain a mailing list of local residents, call up local business which do a lot of direct mailings—realtors are always a good choice—and find out where they obtain their lists. The easiest way to use a mailing list is to purchase it on self adhesive labels. These can be attached to any item you are mailing. I use them on my flyers which I then simply fold, staple, and mail.

The direct mail industry talks about costs in terms of cost per thousand, which is the cost of a thousand items. The cost per thousand for a local mailing list generally will be about $50. You probably will not be mailing enough items to get any bulk rate from the Post Office; therefore, postage will be 29 cents each. For a small mailing, the total cost per thousand, including the mailing list, printing of flyers, and postage, will be about $1000 or $1 per address.

I personally use direct mail on a regular basis to find new clients. I particularly like to do this just before the end of the year. This is the time when people start making New Year's resolutions which frequently involve fitness. I mail out a couple hundred flyers to addresses in wealthy parts of town. I generally get a return rate of almost 1% which yields me three or four prospective clients.

6.6 Advertising in Local Periodicals

An alternative form of advertising to

the distribution of flyers is to place advertisements in local periodicals. The best time to advertise in a local periodical is in the same issue that a story about you appears. The magazine or newspaper advertising department should work with you to position your advertisement as near to the story as possible. Using advertising to accompany a story is particularly important when your telephone number will not appear in the article.

Advertisements in local papers will cost from $50 to several hundred dollars. If you are willing to run the advertisement multiple times, discounts are usually available. You should restrict yourself to local periodicals. National newspapers and magazines, even fitness related ones, will not provide you with a sufficient return to justify the expense.

6.7 Gift Certificates and Coupons

Gift certificates are another great, inexpensive way to promote your business. The biggest market for them are your existing clients who want to give your services to friends or family members. Gift certificates are especially useful around holidays when people are giving gifts and thinking about New Year's resolutions. After all, what better gift is there than the gift of health?

Gift certificates do not need to be fancy. They should include the company name and logo as well as blanks for the number of sessions being given and your signature. Since they are gifts, they should not include the price. While you probably will sell most of them around Christmas and New Year's, they should be general enough to be used any time of year. A sample gift certificate is included in this chapter.

Let your clients know that you have gift certificates available. You may want to offer clients a discount to encourage them to buy certificates. In addition, advertise your gift certificates in your flyers so that non-clients can take advantage of them as well.

Another promotional idea similar to gift certificates is coupons. In Chapter IV, *Getting Clients*, I suggest that you develop a relationship with at least one local fitness-related store. As part of that relationship, you may want to discuss coupons.

Approach the store owner or manager and offer to distribute store coupons to your clients on behalf of the store. After all, you have daily access to a lot of potential customers for the store. Coupons are a great way for the store to generate more business by reaching people who are likely to want to shop there.

On the other hand, from your point of view, giving out coupons is a great way for you to reward existing clients and impress potential clients. It is particularly impressive if the store will create or allow you to create coupons with your company name and logo on them. Even without this, however, coupons are an impressive form of advertisement.

6.8 How to Evaluate Your Advertising

The purpose of advertising is to gain customers—in the case of a personal training business—clients. The purpose is not to see your name in print, or build up your ego, or waste money; although, all too often, that is the result. Smart advertising means evaluating the effectiveness of different types of approaches, continuing those that work, and discontinuing those that do not work. Two tools for assessing effectiveness are the response rate and cost per sale.

6.8.1 Response Rate

Response rate is the percentage of people reached by an advertisement who actually respond to it. For example, suppose that you distribute one thousand flyers in an affluent neighborhood in your area and twenty people respond. Your response rate from that advertisement is 2%. Similarly, if you place an advertisement in a local newspaper which has a circulation of 10,000 and 1 person responds, your response rate from that advertisement is .01%.

The benefit of keeping track of response rates from your advertisements is that it allows you to predict responses from future advertisements. Again, suppose you distribute one thousand flyers in an affluent neighborhood and twenty people respond—a response rate of 2%. Using the response rate, you know that if you distribute another five hundred flyers in the same neighborhood—but to different houses, of course—approximately ten people should respond. In this way, you can test advertisements before you spend a lot of money on them.

This method of estimating future responses is based on two assumptions. First, response rates only are valid for the same type of customers. Make sure, when figuring future responses based on past response rates, that you are dealing with the same type of customers. For example, a response rate based on flyers distributed in an affluent neighborhood would not be valid for flyers distributed in a middle-class neighborhood.

Second, sample size will affect the validity of response rates. Make sure that when you test an advertising technique that you test it on a large enough number of people for the results to be reliable. Ten percent of the target market is usually a good test. In other words, if you want to test a flyer which eventually will be distributed to ten thousand people, a good test would be to distribute it to one thousand people.

6.8.2 Cost Per Sale

Another important measure of the effectiveness of an advertisement is cost per sale. This is a measure of how much it costs you to get each response. Cost per sale is calculated by dividing the total cost of the advertisement by the total number of responses.

For example, if you buy an advertisement in a local paper for $400 and get two responses from it, your cost per sale is $200. If, on the other hand, you place a $4,000 advertisement in a national fitness magazine and you get two usable responses in your area, your cost per sale is $2,000.

Assuming you charge $50 per training session, a cost per sale of $200 for a client who will train once a week on a regular basis is very reasonable. A cost per sale of $2,000 is not. That explains why you see advertisements for personal trainers in local papers but not in national fitness magazines.

The key to advertising wisely is to invest only a little money until you have found a technique that works. Response rate and cost per sale are two measures which provide you with the tools you need to evaluate advertising approaches and make smart and cost-effective advertising decisions.

6.9 What You Need to Know about Printing

The topic of this book is the personal training business, not the publishing business. Nonetheless, occasionally you will need to print certain items— business cards, brochures, flyers, and the like. When you do, you will need the services of a local printer. It is a good idea to have a basic understanding of printing terminology and your printing options so you can communicate with printers and approach them at least somewhat informed.

6.9.1 Illustrations

There are two types of illustrations used in print: line art illustrations and halftone illustrations. Line art illustrations are line drawings and other graphics. Line art cannot represent shades so it cannot reproduce actual photographs. However, used correctly, line art can be as effective—sometimes even more effective—than actual photographs.

Halftone illustrations are used in printed material to reproduce photographs and other images with shading. Halftone illustration uses collections of dots to represent shades. All photographs reproduced in printed material are reproduced using halftones.

I strongly suggest that you include some type of illustration in your flyer. It will catch people's attention and make the flyer more readable. Line art illustrations are the easiest and least expensive to use. If you are a good artist or you know someone who is, you can include an appropriate drawing. If not, collections of clip art are available in books with hundreds of designs to choose from. You will certainly be able to find something suitable. For books of clip art, check with bookstores and art supplies shops. I use line art in my flyers.

If you want to include a halftone illustration, make sure that it is appropriate to the type of clients you are trying to reach. If a photograph of yourself would increase response rates to the advertisement, then by all means include a photograph of yourself. If before and after photographs of a client or a photograph of an attractive male or female model would better serve to catch the attention of prospective clients, use those instead.

6.9.2 Color

There are two types of color used in printing: spot color and process color. Spot color is, as its name suggests, specific colors used in specific spots. For example, suppose you were designing a flyer, and instead of making all the type black, you wanted to add some variety by printing the headline and some of the key phrases in red. That would be spot color; black plus one color, red. Spot color is relatively inexpensive. Using black plus one or two colors is a good, inexpensive way to introduce color into a flyer.

Process color is color used to reproduce actual shades and hues. I mentioned above that halftones are used in printing to reproduce photographs. All color halftones in books, magazines, and any other printed material are printed using process color. Process color is expensive. It is so expensive that it is not cost effective to use process color for the type of flyers typically designed for a personal training business.

While you generally think of inks when you think of color printing, do not forget about paper. Printing on colored paper is another way to use color in a flyer. That is what I do for my flyers. I use one color printing—blank ink—on colored paper. This provides my flyers with color and is very inexpensive.

If you are interested in using color in your flyers, talk to local printers about the costs of the various options. They should be able to tell you very quickly which options are within your budget and which are not. As with other advertising techniques, when you use color, be aware of the response rate. No matter how pretty an advertisement, if using color does not increase response rate, it is a waste of money.

6.9.3 Working with a Printer

If you have a computer with the appropriate software, you may want to typeset your printed material yourself. Otherwise, your local print shop can typeset it for you. If the print shop is doing the typesetting, bring with you a typewritten copy of what you want typeset. Organize the words on the paper approximately how you would like them to appear on the typeset copy. Naturally, the type from your typewriter will not be the same size as the finished type.

If you want line art included—a company logo for a business card or a clip art illustration for a flyer, for example—bring that along with your text. The printer will incorporate it into the final design. If you want a halftone photograph included in the printed material, bring along that as well.

Chapter Seven
Expanding Your Business

After you have been running your personal training business for awhile and making a comfortable living, there may come a time when you want more out of your business. Perhaps you will want to increase your income. Perhaps you will become tired of constantly traveling from client to client and want to hire other trainers. Or, perhaps the initial excitement of starting a business will have worn off and you will need other challenges. If and when this happens, consider expanding your business.

7.1 Hiring Other Trainers

The most obvious way to expand your personal training business is to hire other trainers. Hiring other trainers to work for you will enable your company to handle more clients and bring in more income. Be aware, however, that even under the best of circumstances, with the most reliable and independent of people, you will have to devote some of your time to management issues such as scheduling and pay. This will mean spending less of your time training clients and more of your time managing your trainers. If you want to get away from the daily routine of training clients, this may be ideal. If you do not like administrative work and really just love being with clients, however, you should consider carefully before you start hiring other trainers.

7.1.1 When to Start Hiring

Start hiring additional trainers when you are certain that you have enough business to warrant another trainer, but before you become saturated with clients. Do not wait to hire additional trainers until you have more clients than you can handle; it will be too late. The relationship between trainer and client is very personal. It is difficult to transfer an established client to another trainer. Therefore, do not expect any of the trainers you hire to take over your existing clients; you will need to continue training your existing clients yourself. Plan on finding new clients for any new trainers you hire.

7.1.2 How and Where to Find Suitable Trainers

Probably the biggest challenge when hiring a trainer is finding the right one. A good trainer can enhance your business, increase your income, and free up your time for other tasks. But a bad trainer, one who is unreliable or worse, incompetent, can eat up resources and damage—even destroy—your business. Choosing the right person, therefore, is essential.

The first rule when hiring trainers is the fewer the better. In other words, the fewer people you need to handle your business, the better off you are. Quality not quantity counts; having several reliable trainers is preferable to having many unreliable ones.

One way to find qualified people is to train them yourself. To do this, consider offering a college internship. Although most college students will not have personal training experience, you probably can find some who at least have the requisite knowledge of physiology and kinesiology. Combined with a willingness to learn, this should be sufficient background.

To start an internship program, contact a local college or university and talk to the people in the various departments that deal with physiology and kinesiology. Physical education, physical therapy, and sports medicine majors also are good prospects for interns. Remember that, regardless of the student the school offers, it is your choice whom to take on as an intern. Do not only look for someone who has the necessary knowledge and experience. Also look for someone who has a suitable personality to be a personal trainer, someone, for example, who is good at dealing with people and who can lead clients without being overbearing or obnoxious. See Chapter I, *Becoming a Personal Trainer,* for a discussion of the necessary attributes for being a successful personal trainer. Ultimately, the most important question to ask yourself when evaluating any potential intern is would I want to hire this person?

An internship typically will last for a school semester or a summer. You will need to prepare a brief course of study for the college indicating what the intern will be expected to learn during the internship. A several-page outline of topics to be covered in the course of the internship probably will be sufficient, although the school may have more specific requirements. Putting together this outline will not only benefit the school and the student; it also will be helpful for you when the time comes at the end of the internship to evaluate the intern's progress and decide whether or not you want to hire him or her as a regular trainer.

Once you have found an intern, take him or her around with you as you train your regular clients. Initially, how much you let the intern do will depend on his or her experience and skill level. If nothing else, in the beginning he or she can always help carry equipment. As the intern progresses, however, you should allow him or her gradually to take on more responsibility. Ultimately, your goal is to have the intern doing entire training sessions. Whether or not this happens will depend on how well the intern does and how confident you are in his or her abilities.

Interns work for credit, not for regular pay. In fact, their school may specifically require that they not be paid. If they are paid, it is very little, usually no more than five to ten dollars an hour. Remember, however, that they are not slave labor; they are supposed to be getting something out of working for you. You need to make sure that the internship is a learning experience.

If the intern successfully completes his or her internship requirements and you feel comfortable with him or her as a person, make him or her a job offer. If the intern is not graduating yet, he or she could work part-time during school until graduation. When you do hire a former intern, remember that the intern is now a regular trainer; he or she should be treated and paid as such.

There is one school of thought in management that the way to hire staff is to get the cheapest people you can find and then micro-manage every detail of their work. While this gives the manager a sense of power and may even save money in the short term, it neither is very efficient nor very effective. Not only does it put all the responsibility on the manager, it limits the ability of employees to work to their potential and denies them any real incentive for achieving excellence.

I have always believed that you should hire the best people you can find. Then, you should provide them with goals and motivation to reach those goals, give them the tools they need to succeed, and get out of their way. While this requires delegating responsibility and trusting your employees, ultimately, it proves much more rewarding both for you and for them.

Suppose, for example, you have a choice between hiring a college graduate with a degree in sports medicine and a high school graduate whose only knowledge of exercise is what he has picked up at the gym. Looking just at the short term cost, you might be tempted to hire the high school graduate. After all, with what you pay him an hour, you could make a fortune off the clients he trains. Remember, though, that although the college graduate will cost you more, he or she will be able provide your clients with better, safer workouts. This will be better for your clients—so they will continue to give you their business and tell their friends about your company— and, eventually, better for business.

Even if you hire experienced trainers, you should not do so without first observing them at work. Have the prospective trainer travel around with you for at least several days and train some of your existing clients under your close supervision. They should not be paid for this time since it is part of the interview process and their chance to prove themselves to you. When you are satisfied that a trainer can deliver, the two of you should begin to perform free initial consultations with new clients before he or she starts training them.

7.1.3 Hiring Other Trainers as Contractors

There are two ways to hire trainers to work for you. You can hire them as independent contractors or you can hire them as employees. Both methods have major legal and tax implications.

Ultimately it is the IRS that decides if someone is an employee or an independent contractor. One test the IRS uses to determine the status of an individual who works for you is whether the individual works at your site under your supervision. Since your trainers will not be working at your office or under your direct control, you have a good chance of hiring them as independent contractors. There are, however, some additional procedures you should follow to help ensure the IRS does not treat them as employees.

First, you should have a written contract with the trainer describing the work he or she is to do for you but specifying that you will have no direct control over his or her work. This contract should state that the trainer is not an employee but an independent contractor responsible for providing his or her own equipment and paying his or her own taxes. See the sample contract with an independent trainer in the Forms Section of this book.

In addition to the equipment, you should have the trainer provide his or her own insurance. See Chapter III, *Setting up Your Business*, for a discussion on getting insurance. If you observe these simple rules, you should have no trouble convincing the IRS that the trainer is an independent contractor.

Note that if you hire trainers as outside contractors you will avoid the complicated tax paperwork involved with maintaining employees. However, you still will need to fill out Form 1099-MISC for each trainer at the end of each year. This form tells the trainer and the IRS the amount of money you have paid him or her during the year, money on which he or she is responsible for paying taxes.

Also note that while an independent trainer will be responsible for obtaining liability insurance, you should obtain from the trainer written proof of this insurance. You should have the trainer provide you with a copy of the insurance certificate with your company listed on it as an insured. See Chapter III, *Setting Up Your Business*, for information on doing this. Along with proof of insurance, get proof of any degrees or fitness certifications the trainer may have.

7.1.4 Hiring Other Trainers as Employees

The major complication of hiring trainers as employees, rather than as outside contractors, involves taxation. If you are planning on becoming an employer, get IRS Publication 15, *Employer's Tax Guide,* and Form SS-4, *Application for Employer Identification Number.* Also, check with the department of taxation of your state for the appropriate procedures and forms for withholding and paying state income tax. Your tax duties as an employer will include calculation and withholding of federal income and Social Security tax for each employee, calculation and withholding of state income and disability taxes for each employee, filing payroll tax returns every quarter, payment of the employer's portion of Social Security and unemployment taxes for each employee, and preparation of W-2 forms for each employee.

The other major concern when hiring trainers as employees is insurance. When hiring trainers as contractors, the trainers will be responsible for their own liability insurance. When hiring trainers as employees, however, you will need to provide insurance for them. See Chapter III, *Setting up Your Business,* for a discussion on obtaining insurance coverage for employees.

Also note that, although you are not required at the current time to provide employees with health insurance, health care reforms proposed by the Clinton Administration may require you to do so in the very near future. There has been a great deal of debate over whether these reforms will increase the cost of maintaining employees. The small

business community is almost unanimous in the belief that they will. This is another consideration when deciding whether to hire trainers as employees.

If this brief discussion of the responsibilities of being an employer scares you—it is meant to. I strongly suggest, at least initially, you hire any trainers you need as contractors. You can always make them employees later.

7.1.5 *Non-compete Agreement*

Your trainers are not stupid; if they were, you would not have hired them. They know what you are paying them and what you are charging the clients they train. They will realize that instead of working for you, they could do the same thing for themselves and make twice as much money. In fact, that is one of the points of this book. Eventually, many of your trainers will leave to start their own personal training businesses. This is inevitable. When it happens, you should take it in stride, wish the trainer luck, and find a replacement.

As for the trainer's clients, they are your clients and should remain with your company. Of course, that is easier said than done. Because the client's relationship is with the trainer, not with you, keeping the trainer's clients once the trainer has left the company may be difficult.

Even if you cannot keep the clients, however, you can prevent the trainer from taking them. Whether your trainers are employees or independent contractors, every new trainer should sign a non-compete agreement when he or she comes to work for you. This agreement should specify that the trainer is not allowed to train any of your company's clients for a period of time—perhaps a year—after he or she leaves. At the very least, denying them access to former clients may help discourage your trainers from leaving.

Besides preventing your trainers from leaving and taking your clients, you also want to prevent them from moonlighting—training other clients on the side. When you start hiring trainers, you need to decide if their duties will include finding new clients. You may prefer, as I do, to do all new recruiting yourself. If so, your non-compete agreement should specify that a trainer cannot solicit new clients. On the other hand, you may want to encourage your trainers to find new business for the company. In this case, your non-compete agreement should specify that the trainer is free to find new clients but that all new clients a trainer finds must be brought to you and trained through your company. See the sample non-compete agreement provided.

While, in most cases, you will want to prevent your trainers from taking clients with them when they leave, there is one exception. If you hire experienced trainers—and, as I said above, I encourage you to do so—they may bring with them some of their existing clients. In that case, you may need to make an exception in the non-compete agreement

to allow the trainer to keep those clients if and when he or she leaves. Naturally, this is to the trainer's advantage not yours; so do not offer to do this unless the trainer insists. If you do make an exclusion, make sure it is in writing and specifies exactly which clients are excluded from the non-compete agreement so that there is no room for dispute later.

7.1.5 *Motivating Your Trainers*

As I have said before, motivating your trainers means providing them with clear goals. To do this, you first need to decide what your trainers' goals will be. Then you need to make the trainers aware of these goals. And finally, you need to provide them with incentives for reaching these goals.

As any business owner knows, it is a lot easier to make money from an existing customer than to find a new one. This is as true of the personal training business as it is of any other. Therefore, one of your principal goals, and one of the principal goals of your trainers, probably will be client retention.

You and your trainers should actively work to keep clients. This means varying workouts, providing clients with evidence of their progress, and generally keeping them happy and interested in what they are doing with you.

While the importance of client retention may be obvious to you, it may not be obvious to your trainers. They may be focused elsewhere or not really focused at all. If you have decided that client retention is a primary goal, you need to make this point clear to them. You also need to discuss with them the specific steps they can take to increase client retention.

Of course, if your business is going to grow, retaining existing clients is not sufficient; you also will need to find new clients. Again, you have to actively work to make it happen. As I said before, you may prefer to recruit new clients yourself. Or you may want to involve your trainers in recruiting clients. If you want your trainers involved, you need to make them aware that finding new clients is also one of their goals.

Once your trainers are clear on the goals that you have set for them, you need to provide them with incentives for reaching those goals. If their primary goal is client retention, for example, you might provide your trainers with bonuses based on the length of time they have had each of their clients—the longer they have kept a client, the bigger the bonus. Similarly, if another goal is to find new clients, you might provide your trainers with bonuses for each new client they bring into the company.

Be creative when inventing incentives. While a bonus might be money, it could just as well be something else which would motivate your trainers. For example, paying for certain continuing education courses could be worth more to them than money because, unlike bonuses, the tuition will not be treated as taxable income. Other incentives might be the opportunity to take on more clients or to participate in another interesting company project such as a new product or service.

7.1.6 Managing Your Trainers

Chances are you started your personal training business without any employees and therefore are accustomed to doing everything yourself. When you first start hiring, it will be difficult to delegate tasks to others. If you are going to successfully expand your business, however, you must be willing to let your employees take over some of the work. While you want to maintain control, you do not want to have to micro-manage your trainers. After all, you hired them to save work, not create more of it. Exactly how carefully you will need to monitor your trainers will depend directly on the quality of people you hired.

When you find a new client for one of your trainers, go with your trainer to the initial consultation. You want to make first contact with the client so that he or she knows who you are and feels comfortable calling you if problems arise which your trainer cannot handle or if your trainer becomes a problem. You also want to ensure that the new client is a suitable customer and that he or she is happy with your trainer.

After the initial consultation, you should have no regular contact with the client. Training sessions thereafter should be scheduled with the trainer directly. You may be tempted to do all the scheduling yourself, but you should avoid this temptation. Doing all the scheduling for your own clients as well as those of all your trainers quickly would become too time consuming.

Each of your trainers will need his or her own answering machine and beeper. All appointments, cancellations, and rescheduling should be done directly between client and trainer. You should become personally involved only if a trainer needs a replacement due to sickness or vacation or if a client encounters a problem, such as a question concerning payment, which his or her trainer cannot handle.

Plan on holding a weekly meeting with all your trainers. This meeting will allow you to stay in contact with your trainers and discuss everything from new ideas to scheduling. If the company has some new clients or is embarking on an interesting new project, these meetings will provide the time to discuss these new developments. If a trainer is having a problem with a client or the company is having a problem, it can be discussed at these meetings as well. The most important reason for holding these meetings, however, is to foster a sense of common purpose among your trainers and to keep them motivated and excited about what they are doing.

Although your trainers will do all their own scheduling, you need to make sure that you are being paid. To ensure this, have clients pay their trainers with

checks made out to your company. The trainer should then pass these checks on to you during your weekly meeting. Note that having clients pay in cash or by check made out to the trainer is a recipe for disaster. It is too tempting for a trainer to pocket the money and not tell you about it. Trust your trainers, but do not put temptation in their way.

While clients will pay for a set number of sessions in advance, you should pay trainers on a regular basis, twice a month perhaps, for work already done. Trainers are typically paid 40 to 60 percent of what the client is charged.

Besides checks from clients, have your trainers provide you with a weekly training log for each client which lists the date and time of each training session completed. Compare this log to the checks you have received to make sure that all clients are current in their payments. Also, make it a practice to call up a few clients each week to check that they were trained at the dates and times listed by their trainer and that they are happy with the training sessions. It will make your clients feel important knowing that you care enough to check on how their training is going and will make you feel secure in the knowledge that your trainers are doing their job. As gracefully as possible, let your trainers know that you are making these random checks so it will not come as a suprise to them. Knowing that you are checking up on them will help to keep your trainers on their toes.

Obviously, you need to be tactful

when calling clients. Although one of the reasons for your call is to make sure that the trainer trained the client on the dates he or she claimed, you do not want to give either the client or the trainer the impression that this is why you are calling. Focus your call on making sure that the client is satisfied with the trainer, not whether or not the trainer is being dishonest. In other words, place the emphasis on customer satisfaction, not employee dishonesty. In the unlikely event that your trainer is indeed fabricating training logs, this quickly will become evident without too much prying on your part.

> **"Group programs allow you to increase your clientele without adding more trainers."**

While you want a relationship to be established between your trainer and the client, not between you and the client, let the client know that he or she should feel free to call you if problems or questions arise that his or her trainer cannot resolve. If you hire good, reliable trainers, you should not encounter many problems of this sort. However, by encouraging clients to call you if there is a problem with a trainer who is not doing his or her job, you will hear about it from your clients before it becomes a crisis.

7.2 Running Your Own Group Programs

While hiring additional trainers is the most obvious way to expand your business, it is not the only way. Another option is to supplement your one-on-one training with group programs. Group programs allow you to increase your clientele without adding more trainers. They are easier to manage than additional trainers and generally more lucrative.

If you want to get into doing group programs, the first thing you need to decide is what kinds of programs you will offer. This will depend both on your interests and abilities and the type of customers you want to attract. While the most common type of group program is aerobics, other choices of program types include martial arts, water walking, weight control counseling, and group weight training. In addition, within each of these categories there are specialties. For example, within aerobics there is high impact aerobics, low impact aerobics, step aerobics, jump aerobics, jazzercise, funk aerobics, and probably other types of aerobics which I have forgotten to mention.

The key to deciding which type of program to offer is to find the program that will attract the most people and, if possible, distinguish you from your competition. In Chapter III, *Setting up Your Business*, I describe how to formulate a brief business plan for your personal training business that includes an analysis of the marketplace and the competition. You should put together a similar plan for any group programs or—for that matter—other type of business you decide to get involved in.

7.2.1 *Programs for County Recreation Departments*

I have found that the easiest way to start a group program is to offer one for a local county recreation department. Almost all counties in the country offer some types of recreation programs. You have probably seen their catalogs. They offer classes on everything from basket weaving to using computers. Health and fitness courses also usually are included among the course offerings.

Start by getting the catalog for your local county and see what courses they offer. If possible, you should look for a course to offer which is not already available. When I began offering these types of programs, for example, there were a lot of aerobics classes. No one was offering step aerobics, however. So, naturally, I started some step classes.

Besides deciding on the type of program to offer, you also will need to decide how much to charge. Again, use the catalog as a guide. See what other programs cost and price your program accordingly. If you are offering a special type of program that no one else offers, you probably can price your program slightly higher than average. If you are offering a program for which there is competition, you should stay with the going price, perhaps even undercut it if you feel you can safely do so and still make a profit.

Once you have decided the type of class to offer and the fee you want to charge, call up the county Parks and Recreation Department. You can find their telephone number in the local government listings in your telephone book. When you call, you probably will be referred to the department's fitness director. As with getting into gyms and health clubs, know what you want to say and be ready with credentials and references.

Working for a county is very easy. The county will provide you with a free listing in their catalog so you will not need to advertise. They also will handle program registration, cancellations, and fees. They will keep approximately 25% of the program fee they take in and pay you the rest. Let me give you one word of caution: when dealing with the government, receiving payment is slow. You usually will not be paid until the end of the entire program—typically several weeks. Plan accordingly.

If you have the expertise and interest, you can offer these group programs yourself. Otherwise, you can hire instructors to give them for you. My company, for example, offers aerobics programs through the local county. While I could teach these classes myself, I prefer to hire aerobics instructors to teach them for me. This is my instructors' area of expertise, not mine; hiring instructors to do the aerobics classes allows me to concentrate on what I do best, one-on-one personal training, and ensures that the people who take my aerobics classes get the best instruction possible.

For aerobics, instructors are generally paid around $10 to $15 a session. Again, I try to get the best possible people I can find so I pay a little more: $25 to $30 a session.

7.2.2 *Programs for Businesses*

While working with county recreation departments is probably the easiest way to develop group programs, the fastest growing and ultimately most lucrative way to start a group program is to work with businesses such as large corporations. Corporate programs can consist of anything from managing a fitness facility within an office building to holding aerobics classes in a conference room. Corporate America loses millions of dollars a year as a result of employee absenteeism. Corporations have a big incentive to provide employees with fitness programs. Such programs can reduce health insurance premiums as well as improve employee health and morale.

The downside to becoming involved with corporations is that it is not easy to get your foot in the door, especially if you are a small company. If you are extremely motivated and persistent, however, you may see results. It will be worth the effort. Becoming associated with a single corporation can literally double your business. Choose a few corporations in your area and contact the human resources or personnel office.

7.2.3 *Your Own Programs*

An alternative to creating programs for the county or a business is to create programs entirely on your own. Doing so will provide you with complete control over what you do and when you do it. It also will enable you to keep all the income from the program. There is a downside, however. You must provide your own space in which to run the program. You must handle your own advertising and publicity. And, you must handle your own program registration and all other related details. Some trainers find organizing their own programs extremely rewarding and worthwhile. Others find that the disadvantages outweigh the advantages.

If you decide to organize your own programs, unless you already have a space large enough, you will have to find somewhere to run them. You may be able to find a fitness business such as an equipment store that will let you use some space for free in return for bringing in customers. Most likely, however, you will have to rent space.

One of the best places to rent space for these types of programs is in local public schools. Although you may not be aware of this, most public elementary and secondary schools rent space in their facilities for after hour activities. Schools are good places to run fitness programs because the space is relatively inexpensive and they generally are located in residential areas. In some places, school space is in such demand that you may have to try several different schools before you find one with the accommodations that you need.

School classrooms generally will rent for under $30 per hour. Larger rooms such as gyms and auditoriums obviously cost more. Contact the business offices of local schools or local Board of Education for more information on renting space. You will find telephone numbers for local public schools in the local government section of your telephone book.

Besides obtaining space in which to run the program, you also will need to advertise to make people aware of the program you are offering. Flyers are probably the best choice for this. See Chapter VI, *Advertising and Publicity*, for a discussion on how to create and distribute flyers. If you are running a program in a school, consider distributing flyers to school children to take home to their parents. Naturally, this should be done with the permission of the school. Advertisements in local papers also may be useful for publicizing your program. But do not ignore free publicity. Local papers always are looking for stories; getting an article placed in a local publication would be a great way to get the word out about your program. Again, see Chapter VI for more information on using the news media to publicize your business.

7.2.4 Insurance and Group Waiver Form

If and when you offer group pro-

grams, you need to ensure that your business is covered by liability insurance for this purpose. If you are giving a program for a county Parks and Recreation Department or a private business, you may be covered under their insurance. Do not assume this, however; make sure. If you are not covered or if you are offering a program on your own, give your insurance broker a call and make sure that the type of group programs you are planning to offer are covered under your policy. If they are not covered, obtain a rider to the policy to cover the specific programs.

As with one-on-one training, in addition to insurance, you should have all clients sign a waiver form as part of registration for the program. While this can be a separate form, if this is your own program and you are handling the registration yourself, it is better to incorporate the waiver into the program registration form. A sample group waiver form is included in this chapter.

7.3 Selling Merchandise

I have said before that it is easier to an additional product to an existing customer than to find a new customer. Your existing clients not only are a source of continuing income from training sessions; they also represent excellent customers for additional products or services. This is particularly true if you are running group programs that attract a lot of people. Therefore, as you are looking for ways to expand your business, you may want to consider selling merchandise to your clients.

7.3.1 Choosing a Product to Sell

The most obvious product to sell clients is exercise equipment. Many of your clients will be working out at home and will need weights and other equipment.

In Chapter IV, *Getting Clients*, I mentioned the usefulness of having a relationship with a fitness equipment store in order to get leads on potential clients. It is also useful to have a relationship with a store which allows you to purchase equipment for clients. If you want to resell equipment to clients, develop a relationship with at least one fitness equipment store. When a client needs equipment, you will purchase it from the store for the client. The store should give you commercial pricing—approximately 10% below retail. You can either pass this savings along to your client or add a markup for yourself. Whatever price you ultimately charge the client, however, make sure it is not more than the price the client would have paid had he or she purchased the equipment directly him or herself. The client should pay you for the equipment, and you should pay the store.

Other products you might want to consider selling to clients include clothing, such as workout wear and aerobic wear, and nutritional supplements, such as vitamins, protein drinks, and energy drinks. Anything that would be of

interest to your clients and is related to health, fitness, or exercise is a possibility.

Whatever product you decide to sell, let me give you this caution: make sure it is something of real value to the client. Remember that you are a personal trainer; your primary responsibility is to improve your clients' health and fitness, not sell them things they do not need. Do not force a product on a client just to make a buck.

7.3.2 Buying Products to Sell

All of the products mentioned above are available wholesale from many manufacturers and distributors. Exercise and fitness magazines frequently have advertisements from manufacturers and distributors looking for retailers. Also check with local gyms, health food stores, and fitness stores and find out who their distributors are.

As an alternative, if you are inventive, you may want to develop your own product. After all, you have been in the fitness business for awhile and probably have some ideas of your own. One easy product to develop yourself is clothing. Consider creating an interesting design and having it put onto ready-made fitness wear. Some companies even sell clothing with their company name and logo on it. See Chapter III, *Setting up Your Business*, for further discussion. People who buy the clothing are then effectively paying for the privilege of advertising the company. Think about that next time you see someone wearing clothing which says Weider or Nike on it.

Wherever you decide to get your merchandise from, avoid becoming involved in pyramid schemes or other similar marketing arrangements which focus on recruiting people to become distributors rather than on selling a product. Nutritional supplements and cosmetics are two products that have traditionally been popular with pyramid marketers. Take care when looking for products to resell and make sure you are dealing with reputable manufacturers and distributors.

7.3.3 Selling the Product

Once you have found a product to sell, the most obvious customers are your personal training clients. If you are running group classes, you have a ready-made market. For example, suppose you are currently running group aerobic classes. Try selling some aerobic wear after class.

Another way to sell your product is through local gyms and retailers. Naturally, your product has to be something unique that is not available from other suppliers. If this is the case, talk to the managers of local gyms and sporting good stores.

Finally, you might consider selling the product by direct mail. Direct mail is a major distribution channel for exercise and fitness products; with the right product, direct mail can be very effective. If you are interested in pursuing this method of marketing, there are many excellent books on selling products via direct mail. For more information, check with local bookstores and libraries. Also, find your local direct mail association. These are associations of businesses that use direct mail and exchange information about the direct mail business through local meetings and publications. Getting involved with a local direct mail association can be extremely useful for anyone starting out in direct mail.

7.4 Sales Tax License

Almost every state charges sales tax on sales of merchandise. This tax varies from 5% to 10% of the sale price. Even in states where services such as personal training are exempt, if you start selling merchandise, you probably will have to start collecting sales tax.

To do this, you will need to obtain a Sales Tax License, sometimes called a Seller's Permit, from the state. The Sales Tax License not only allows you to collect sales tax. It also allows you to buy wholesale goods for resale without paying tax. If you are selling aerobic wear, for example, and you buy the clothing from someone else, simply by providing your permit number to the seller, you will not be required to pay sales tax on the items you buy for resale.

Once you have a Sales Tax License, whenever you make a sale to anyone in your state, you will need to keep track of the amount of sales tax collected. Sales tax is recorded on your income ledger which is discussed in Chapter III, *Setting up Your Business.* You then will have to remit the tax you have collected to the state. Currently, sales tax only needs to be collected on sales within your state. If you are running a mail order operation, for example, and you make a sale to someone in another state, you do not need to collect sales tax on the sale.

To apply for a Sales Tax License, contact your state's sales tax office. You can find their telephone number in the local government listings in your telephone book. When you apply for a Sales Tax License, you will be sent detailed information on how to collect and pay sales tax.

Be aware that to obtain a Sales Tax License you may need to provide a deposit. This deposit can vary from a few hundred dollars to a few thousand dollars. The amount is negotiable. If you cannot pay it, contact the tax office and let them know. After all, they have an incentive to allow you to obtain a Sales Tax License since, if you cannot get one, you cannot collect and pay sales tax.

7.5 Merchant's Account

If the only service your business offers is personal training, accepting payment by check is probably sufficient. When you start selling merchandise, however, you may want to accept credit card payment as well. This is particularly useful if you are selling by mail. Allowing customers to pay by credit

card will increase sales and decrease the number of bad checks you will receive.

The most widely used credit cards are Visa, Mastercard, Discover, and American Express. To accept any of these cards, you will need to open a credit card merchant's account at a bank which offers this service. Some banks offer merchant's accounts for all four types of credit cards. Other banks only offer Visa/Mastercard merchant's accounts.

When you approach banks about this service, be aware that they generally are extremely reluctant to open credit card merchant's accounts for new, non-retail businesses. There are too many dishonest mail-order operators who obtain merchant's accounts, pass unauthorized charges through them, and then disappear. For this reason, many banks will not even consider offering a merchant's account to a business which does not have a storefont and has not been in business at least a year. Developing a relationship with a local bank, as I suggest you do in Chapter III, is the best way to ensure that you will be able to obtain a merchant's account when you need one.

When you open a merchant's account, the bank will provide you with instructions and equipment for authorizing charges and printing charge slips. If the bank uses electronic credit card terminals, you will need to purchase or lease one of these units from the bank. These units typically cost several hundred dollars to purchase and $30 or $40 dollars per month to rent. In addition to the cost of the equipment, the bank will take a percentage—usually 2 or 3%—of all credit card payments you receive.

Although being able to accept credit cards is most useful for selling merchandise, once you are set up to handle credit card sales, you can accept credit cards from other types of customers also. For example, once you have a merchant's account, you can allow your one-on-one personal training clients to pay by credit card. And, if you are offering group programs, you can allow people registering for the programs to pay by credit card as well.

Afterword
Doing It

Nothing in this world can take the place of persistence. Talent will not; nothing is more common than unsuccessful people with talent. Genius will not; unrewarded genius is almost a proverb. Education will not; the world is full of educated derelicts. Persistence and determination alone are omnipotent. The slogan "press on" has solved and always will solve the problems of the human race.

- Calvin Coolidge

What are the ingredients of success? Intelligence, talent, luck—these are all important elements of success. But there are many intelligent, talented, lucky people in this world who have never achieved their goals. The key ingredient of success—without which the others are useless—is persistence. Success in most endeavors depends as much on hard work—getting out there and just doing it, to paraphrase a popular advertising slogan—as it does on anything else.

If you want to consider starting a personal training business, you will hear about and meet a lot of people who claim to be personal trainers. Some of them will have successful businesses; most will not. This is not because they are not capable of running a successful personal training business; this is because they have not put in the time, energy, and commitment necessary to be successful.

It is relatively easy to just train a few clients and be content. It is relatively easy to spend free time day-dreaming about having a big personal training business rather than going out and actually making it happen. It is easy to read a book about starting a personal training business. It is another thing to actually make it happen.

If you are not willing to do what it takes, then you are not sincerely committed to running your own personal training business. If this is the case, as I said before, you should consider working for someone else.

If you are serious about starting your personal training business, you now have the necessary tools. I have told you what you need to know or where to find what you need to know. If you follow the steps laid out in this book, you can be successful. But you have to do it. Just reading this book is not enough; you have to take action.

This book is an outgrowth of the work I have done over the last few years advising other personal trainers on how to start personal training businesses. It is always very exciting for me to see someone I have helped become successful. I have developed a collection of business cards of people I have helped over the years. When you start your business, send me one of your business cards, and let me know how you are doing. If you have other comments, suggestions, or criticisms of this book, I welcome those as well. You can write me care of Willow Creek Publications at the following address:

Ed Gaut
c/o Willow Creek Publications
P.O. Box 86032
Gaithersburg, MD 20886

I have given you the basic tools and information you need to be successful. Now, it is up to you to supply the motivation, the creativity, and the patience to persevere and to succeed. I wish you the best of luck.

Forms

This section contains the reproducable forms referenced elsewhere in the book. Before using a form, I suggest that you photocopy it and use the copy. This will preserve the original form in the book for future use.

Business Plan Worksheet

Objectives and Goals

Describe the objectives and goals you have for your personal training business:

_____

_____

_____

_____

_____

_____

_____

_____

How many clients do you expect the business to have:

1st year _____   2nd year _____   5th year _____

How much gross income (income before expenses) do you expect the business to generate:

1st year _____   2nd year _____   5th year _____

How many contractors and/or employees do you expect to have:

1st year _____   2nd year _____   5th year _____

Target Customers

Describe who your target customers are:

Age   _____

Sex   _____

Income   _____

Education   _____

Marital status   _____

Geographic location   _____

Age   _____

Sex   _____

Income   _____

Education   _____

Marital status   _____

Geographic location   _____

Age   _____

Sex   _____

Income   _____

Education   _____

Marital status   _____

Geographic location   _____

List other characteristics of your target customers:

_____

_____

_____

_____

_____

_____

_____

Services

Describe the services you will offer your customers and how much you will charge for these services:

_____

_____

_____

_____

_____

_____

_____

Competition

List your major competitors:

_____

_____

_____

_____

_____

_____

List the services your competitors offer and how much they charge for these services:

_____

_____

_____

_____

_____

_____

_____

List the ways in which your competitors market their services:

_____

_____

_____

_____

_____

_____

_____

Marketing Plan

List the ways in which you will market your services:

_____

_____

_____

_____

_____

_____

_____

Check each of the following techniques you will use to market your services:

☐ Referals from doctors

☐ Referals from fitness stores

☐ Free programs

☐ News releases

☐ News stories

☐ Flyers

☐ Advertisements in local newspapers

☐ Gift certificates

☐ Coupons

Income Worksheet

	1	2	3	4	5	6	7	8	9	10	11	12
Number of clients												
Number of sessions per week per client												
Number of sessions per week												
Number of weeks per month												
Number of sessions per month												
Fee per session												
Gross income per month												
Total gross income												

Expense Worksheet

Date _____

	1	2	3	4	5	6	7	8	9	10	11	12
Advertising Expenses												
Automobile Expenses												
Insurance												
Office expenses												
Supplies												
Utilities												
Company Uniform												
Monthly Totals												
Total Expenses												

Profit and Loss Worksheet

Date _____

	1	2	3	4	5	6	7	8	9	10	11	12
Total Gross Income per month (from Income Worksheet)												
Total Expenses per month (from Expense Worksheet)												
Net Income per Month												
Total Net Income												

Waiver and Release of All Claims by Client

The CLIENT acknowleges that any program of fitness exercise involves a risk of injury.

The CLIENT represents that he/she has been recently examined by a medical doctor and been found able to undertake a program of exercise.

For and in consideration of the design of an exercise program for CLIENT by _____ ("TRAINER"), CLIENT agrees:

    1. that any exercise program shall be undertaken by CLIENT at his/her sole risk; and

    2. that TRAINER shall not be liable to CLIENT, nor any other person, for any claims or causes of action whatsoever arising out of or connected with the services of TRAINER; and

    3. that CLIENT hereby releases and discharges TRAINER from any such claims or actions.

_____

(signature of CLIENT)

_____

(Date)

Invoice for Personal Training

Company _____

Address _____

_____

Phone _____

Date _____

Invoice Number _____

Client _____

Address _____

_____

_____ training sessions at _____ a session   _____

Sales tax   _____

Total due   _____

Invoice for Merchandise

Company _____

Address _____

_____

Phone _____

Date _____

Invoice Number _____

Client   _____

Address   _____

_____

Quantity	Item	Unit Price	Total Price
_____	_____	_____	_____
_____	_____	_____	_____
_____	_____	_____	_____
_____	_____	_____	_____

Sales Tax   _____

Total Due   _____

Past Due Notice

Company _____

Address _____

_____

Phone _____

Date _____

Client _____

Address _____

_____

Payment for the following invoice(s) is past due:

Invoice Number	Invoice Date	Invoice Amount
_____	_____	_____
_____	_____	_____
_____	_____	_____
_____	_____	_____

Total due _____

Income Ledger   Month _____ Year _____

Post Date	Sale Period	Non-Taxable Sales	Taxable Sales	Sales Tax	Total Sale

Expense Ledger   Month _____   Year _____

Date	Check Number	Payee	Advertising	Automobile	Insurance	Office Expenses

Supplies	Utilities			Total Expenses

How to Get IRS Forms and Publications

You can visit your local IRS office or order tax forms and publications from the IRS Forms Distribution Center listed for your state at the address below. Or, if you prefer, you can photocopy tax forms from reproducible copies kept at participating public libraries. In addition, many of these libraries have reference sets of IRS publications that you can read or copy.

If you are located in:

Alaska, Arizona, California, Colorado, Hawaii, Idaho, Kansas, Montana, Nevada, New Mexico, Oklahoma, Oregon, Utah, Washington, Wyoming, Guam, Northern Marianas, American Samoa

Alabama, Arkansas, Illinois, Indiana, Iowa, Kentucky, Louisiana, Michigan, Minnesota, Mississippi, Missouri, Nebraska, North Dakota, Ohio, South Dakota, Tennessee, Texas, Wisconsin

Connecticut, Delaware, District of Columbia, Florida, Georgia, Maine, Maryland, Massachusetts, New Hampshire, New Jersey, New York, North Carolina, Pennsylvania, Rhode Island, South Carolina, Vermont, Virginia, West Virginia

Send to "Forms Distribution Center" for your state

Western Area Distribution Center
Rancho Cordova, CA
95743-0001

Central Area Distribution Center
P.O. Box 8903
Bloomington, IL
61702-8903

Eastern Area Distribution Center
P.O. Box 85074
Richmond, VA
23261-5074

Foreign Addresses—Taxpayers with mailing addresses in foreign countries should send their requests for forms and publications to:
Eastern Area Distribution Center
P.O. Box 85074
Richmond, VA 23261-5074
or
Western Area Distribution Center
Rancho Cordova, CA
95743-0001,
whichever is closer.

Puerto Rico
Eastern Area Distribution Center
P.O. Box 85074
Richmond, VA 23261-5074

Virgin Islands
V.I. Bureau of Internal Revenue
Lockharts Garden, No. 1A
Charlotte Amalie, St. Thomas
VI 00802

Detach at This Line

- -

Order Blank

We will send you 2 copies of each form and 1 copy of each publication or set of instructions you circle. Please cut the order blank on the dotted line above and **be sure to print or type your name and address accurately on the bottom portion.**

Enclose this order blank in your own envelope and address your envelope to the IRS address shown above for your state.

To help reduce waste, please order only the forms, instructions, and publications you think you will need to prepare your return.

Use the blank spaces to order items not listed. If you need more space, attach a separate sheet of paper listing the additional forms and publications you may need.

You should either receive your order or notification of the status of your order within 7-15 work days after we receive your request.

1040	Schedule F (1040)	1040EZ	3903 & instructions	8829 & Instructions	Pub. 508	Pub. 575	
Instructions for 1040 & Schedules	Schedule R (1040) & instructions	Instructions for 1040EZ	4562 & instructions	Pub. 1	Pub. 521	Pub. 590	
Schedules A&B (1040)	Schedule SE (1040)	1040-ES (1994) & Instructions	4868 & Instructions	Pub. 17	Pub. 523	Pub. 596	
Schedule C (1040)	1040A	1040X & Instructions	5329 & Instructions	Pub. 334	Pub. 525	Pub. 910	
Schedule C-EZ (1040)	Instructions for 1040A & Schedules	2106 & Instructions	8283 & Instructions	Pub. 463	Pub. 527	Pub. 917	
Schedule D (1040)	Schedule 1 (1040A)	2119 & Instructions	8582 & Instructions	Pub. 501	Pub. 529	Pub. 929	
Schedule E (1040)	Schedule 2 (1040A)	2210 & Instructions	8606 & Instructions	Pub. 502	Pub. 550	Pub. 936	
Schedule EIC (1040A or 1040)	Schedule 3 (1040A) & Instructions	2441 & Instructions	8822 & Instructions	Pub. 505	Pub. 554		

Name

Number and street

City or town   State   ZIP code

122

List of Tax Publications for Business Taxpayers

General Guides

1 . . . . . . Your Rights as a Taxpayer
17 . . . . . Your Federal Income Tax (For Individuals)
225 . . Farmer's Tax Guide
334 . . Tax Guide for Small Business
509 . . Tax Calendars for 1994
553 . . Highlights of 1993 Tax Changes
595 . . Tax Guide for Commercial Fishermen
910 . . Guide to Free Tax Services

Employer's Guides

15 . . . . . Employer's Tax Guide (Circular E)
51 . . . . . Agricultural Employer's Tax Guide (Circular A)
80 . . . . . Federal Tax Guide for Employers in the Virgin Islands, Guam, American Samoa, and the Commonwealth of the Northern Mariana Islands (Circular SS)

Specialized Publications

349 . . Federal Highway Use Tax on Heavy Vehicles
378 . . Fuel Tax Credits and Refunds
463 . . Travel, Entertainment, and Gift Expenses
505 . . Tax Withholding and Estimated Tax
510 . . Excise Taxes for 1994
515 . . Withholding of Tax on Nonresident Aliens and Foreign Corporations
517 . . Social Security and Other Information for Members of the Clergy and Religious Workers
527 . . Residential Rental Property
533 . . Self-Employment Tax
534 . . Depreciation
535 . . Business Expenses
536 . . Net Operating Losses
537 . . Installment Sales
538 . . Accounting Periods and Methods
541 . . Tax Information on Partnerships
542 . . Tax Information on Corporations
544 . . Sales and Other Dispositions of Assets
551 . . Basis of Assets
556 . . Examination of Returns, Appeal Rights, and Claims for Refund
557 . . Tax-Exempt Status for Your Organization
560 . . Retirement Plans for the Self-Employed
561 . . Determining the Value of Donated Property
578 . . Tax Information for Private Foundations and Foundation Managers
583 . . Taxpayers Starting a Business
587 . . Business Use of Your Home
589 . . Tax Information on S Corporations
594 . . Understanding The Collection Process
597 . . Information on the United States-Canada Income Tax Treaty
598 . . Tax on Unrelated Business Income of Exempt Organizations
686 . . Certification for Reduced Tax Rates in Tax Treaty Countries
908 . . Bankruptcy and Other Debt Cancellation
909 . . Alternative Minimum Tax for Individuals
911 . . Tax Information for Direct Sellers
917 . . Business Use of a Car
924 . . Reporting of Real Estate Transactions to IRS
925 . . Passive Activity and At-Risk Rules
926 . . Employment Taxes for Household Employers
937 . . Employment Taxes and Information Returns
938 . . Real Estate Mortgage Conduits (REMICs) Reporting Information
946 . . How To Begin Depreciating Your Property
953 . . International Tax Information for Business
1544 . . Reporting Cash Payments of Over $10,000
1546 . . How to use the Problem Resolution Program of the IRS

Spanish Language Publications

1SP . . Derechos del Contribuyente
556SP . . Revisión de las Declaraciones de Impuesto, Derecho de Apelación y Reclamaciones de Reembolsos
579SP . . Cómo Preparar la Declaración de Impuesto Federal
594SP . . Comprendiendo el Proceso de Cobro
850 . . English–Spanish Glossary of Words and Phrases Used in Publications Issued by the Internal Revenue Service

Tax forms, publications and instructions listed on the order blank

You can get the following forms, schedules, and instructions at participating banks, post offices, or libraries.

Form 1040
Instructions for Form 1040 & Schedules
Schedule A for itemized deductions
Schedule B for interest and dividend income if over $400; and for answering the foreign accounts or foreign trusts questions

Schedule EIC for the earned income credit
Form 1040A
Instructions for Form 1040A & Schedules
Schedule 1 for Form 1040A filers to report interest and dividend income

Schedule 2 for Form 1040A filers to report child and dependent care expenses
Form 1040EZ
Instructions for Form 1040EZ

You can photocopy the items listed below (as well as those listed above) at participating libraries or order them from the IRS.

Schedule 3, Credit for the Elderly or the Disabled for Form 1040A Filers
Schedule C, Profit or Loss From Business
Schedule C-EZ, Net Profit From Business
Schedule D, Capital Gains and Losses
Schedule E, Supplemental Income and Loss
Schedule F, Profit or Loss From Farming
Schedule R, Credit for the Elderly or the Disabled
Schedule SE, Self-Employment Tax
Form 1040-ES, Estimated Tax for Individuals
Form 1040X, Amended U.S. Individual Income Tax Return
Form 2106, Employee Business Expenses
Form 2119, Sale of Your Home
Form 2210, Underpayment of Estimated Tax by Individuals and Fiduciaries
Form 2441, Child and Dependent Care Expenses

Form 3903, Moving Expenses
Form 4562, Depreciation and Amortization
Form 4868, Application for Automatic Extension of Time To File U.S. Individual Income Tax Return
Form 5329, Return for Additional Taxes Attibutable to Qualified Retirement Plans, Annuities, and Modified Endowment Contracts
Form 8283, Noncash Charitable Contributions
Form 8582, Passive Activity Loss Limitations
Form 8606, Nondeductible IRA Contributions, IRA Basis, and Nontaxable IRA Distributions
Form 8822, Change of Address
Form 8829, Expenses for Business Use of Your Home
Pub. 501, Exemptions, Standard Deduction, and Filing Information

Pub. 502, Medical and Dental Expenses
Pub. 505, Tax Withholding and Estimated Tax
Pub. 508, Educational Expenses
Pub. 521, Moving Expenses
Pub. 523, Selling Your Home
Pub. 525, Taxable and Nontaxable Income
Pub. 529, Miscellaneous Deductions
Pub. 550, Investment Income and Expenses
Pub. 554, Tax Information for Older Americans
Pub. 575, Pension and Annuity Income
Pub. 590, Individual Retirement Arrangements (IRAs)
Pub. 596, Earned Income Credit
Pub. 910, Guide to Free Tax Services (includes a list of publications)
Pub. 929, Tax Rules for Children and Dependents
Pub. 936, Limits on Home Mortgage Interest Deduction

Medical History Form

First Name _____ Last Name _____

Date of Birth _____ Age _____

Level of Activity (check one):

☐ Sedentary   ☐ Mildly Active   ☐ Active   ☐ Very Active

Notes on Activity _____

_____

_____

Measurements:

Height _____   Weight _____   Body Fat % _____   Body Fat % Goal _____

Arm _____   Thigh _____   Calf _____   Chest _____   Waist _____

Daily Meals:

Breakfast _____

Lunch _____

Dinner_____

Snack(s) _____

Diets:

Have you ever used any diet shakes/pills?   ☐ Yes ☐ No

If yes, what was the result? _____

Hypertension:

Have you ever been diagosed with high blood pressure?   □ Yes □ No

Have you ever been prescribed medication to control
high blood presure?   □ Yes □ No

If yes, explain _____

Smoking:

Do you smoke?   □ Yes □ No

If no, did you ever smoke? How long ago? _____   □ Yes □ No

If yes, how much do/did you smoke? _____

If you smoke, do you want to quit?   □ Yes □ No

Heart:

Have you ever been diagnosed with heart problems?   □ Yes □ No

Do you suffer from chest pain?   □ Yes □ No

Do you ever feel faint or have spells of dizziness?   □ Yes □ No

Have you ever been prescribed medication for heart
problems?   □ Yes □ No

If yes, explain _____

Joints:

Have you ever been diagnosed with joint or soft tissue
probems?   □ Yes □ No

If yes, explain _____

Do you have any problems with your:

    Upper Back   □ Yes □ No
    Lower Back   □ Yes □ No
    Neck   □ Yes □ No
    Shoulders   □ Yes □ No
    Elbows   □ Yes □ No
    Wrists   □ Yes □ No
    Hips   □ Yes □ No
    Knees   □ Yes □ No
    Ankles   □ Yes □ No

If yes, explain _____

In Case of Emergency Contact:

Name _____ Phone Number _____

Pysician:

Name _____ Phone Number _____

Medications Currently Being Used:

_____

_____

_____

Client Training Log

Client Name _____   Month ___ Year ___

Date

Exercise														

Contract with an Independent Trainer

AGREEMENT entered into as of the _____ day of _____, 19_____, by and between _____ (hereinafter referred to as the "Company"), located at _____, and _____ (hereinafter referred to as the "Trainer"), located at _____.

WHEREAS, the Company has certain clients who wish to obtain the services of a personal trainer; and

WHEREAS, Trainer has the professional qualifications and experience to perform independently the services of a personal trainer; and

WHEREAS, the Company and the Trainer desire to set forth in writing the terms and conditions of their agreements and understandings.

HOW, THEREFORE, in consideration of the foregoing, of the mutual promises herein contained, and of other good and valuable consideration, the receipt and sufficiency of which are hereby acknowledged, the parties hereto, intending legally to be bound, hereby agree as follows:

1. Performance by Trainer. The Company shall refer to Trainer clients of the Company who wish to have the services of a personal trainer. Trainer shall arrange to provide the services to the client at such times and places as shall be arranged between Trainer and client. The services shall be performed in a professional manner and shall cover at least the following activities:

_____

_____

_____

_____

2. Term of Contract. The term of this contract (the "Term") shall commence as of the _____ day of _____, 19 ___ and shall continue until either the Company or the Trainer shall provide _____ days written notice to the other of its desire to terminate.

3. Compensation. As and for Trainer's performance and subject to compliance by the Trainer with all of the Trainer's representations, covenants, and agreements set forth in this Agreement, the Company shall pay the Trainer _____ dollars per hour for each hour of services Trainer performs for or on behalf or the Company. Payment shall be made once every _____ for any and all work done for the Company during the prior _____.

4. Independent Contractor. The Trainer shall at all times be an independent contractor hereunder, and not a co-venturer, agent, employee or representative of the Company, and no act, action or omission to act of the Trainer shall in any way be binding upon or obligate the Company. It is understood and agreed by the parties hereto that the Trainer is not an employee for tax purposes. The Trainer hereby represents and warrants to the Company that the Trainer is an independent contractor for all purposes and hereby covenants and agrees to pay any and all taxes required by law to be paid by an independent contractor. [The Trainer shall provide the equipment necessary to carry out the services to be provided.]

5. Noncompetition. During the Term of this agreement and for a period of _____ months after its termination, the Trainer shall not, alone or with others, directly or indirectly, solicit or contact any client of the Company for any purpose, [nor shall the trainer, alone or with others, engage in any business of same or of similar nature to the business of the Company within a _____ mile radius of the Company's place of business as set forth above.] As used in this section 5, the term "client" means any corporation, company, or individual for which the Company, its employees, or its contractors has provided Services during the Term of this contract.

6. Liability. The training performed under this Agreement will be performed entirely at the Trainer's risk and the Trainer agrees to indemnify the Company for any and all liability or loss arising in any way out of the performance of this Agreement. The Trainer will carry, for the duration of this Agreement and at the Trainer's expense, comprehensive general liaility insurance in the amount of _____ dollars on which the Company is named as an additional insured. The Trainer agrees to provide the Company with certificates evidencing the required coverage and policy endorsement before the Trainer begins training hereunder and at the time of renewal of the policy. Trainer will provide the Company with 60 days written notice prior to cancellation or modification of such insurance policy.

7. Miscellany. This Agreement represents the entire understanding by and between the parties. No change or modification hereof shall be valid or binding unless the same is in writing and signed by the party intended to be bound. No waiver of any provision of this Agreement shall be valid unless the same is in writing and signed by the party against whom such waiver is sought to be enforced. No valid waiver of any provision of this Agreement at any time shall be deemed a waiver of any other provision of this Agreement at such time or shall be deemed a valid waiver of such provision at any other time. This Agreement shall be binding on and shall inure to the benefit of the Company and the Trainer, and their respective heirs, personal and legal representatives, successors, and assigns. This Agreement shall be governed by the laws of the State of _____.

IN WITNESS WHEREOF, the Company and the Trainer have duly executed this Agreement as of the day and year set forth above.

COMPANY: TRAINER:

_____   _____
Company Name   Trainer's signature

By _____
   Authorized Signatory, Title

Instructions for Contract with an Independent Trainer

- Initial paragraph. Specify the current date, the name of your company, the address of your company, the name of the trainer, and the address of the trainer.

- Paragraph 1. List the principal activities which the trainer will perform for or on behalf of the company.

- Paragraph 2. Specify the date the contract is to begin and how many days written notice you and the trainer must give each other when terminating the contract.

- Paragraph 3. Specify how much and how often the trainer will be paid.

- Paragraph 4. In order to establish to the satisfaction of the IRS that a trainer is an independent contractor and not an employee, it is important that the trainer provide his or her own equipment. If, in spite of this, you decide to provide equipment for the trainer, cross out the phrase in square brackets.

- Paragraph 5. Specify for how many months after leaving your company the trainer is restricted from soliciting business from your clients.

- Paragraph 5. If in addition to restricting the trainer from soliciting business from your clients you also want to restrict the trainer from training anyone within a certain area, specify within how many miles of your business the trainer is forbidden to train. Otherwise, cross out the phrase in square brackets.

- Paragraph 6. Specify the amount of liability coverage the trainer must carry.

- Paragraph 7. Specify the state in which your business is located.

Form **SS-4**
(Rev. April 1991)
Department of the Treasury
Internal Revenue Service

Application for Employer Identification Number

(For use by employers and others. Please read the attached instructions before completing this form.)

EIN

OMB No. 1545-0003
Expires 4-30-94

Please type or print clearly.

1 Name of applicant (True legal name) (See instructions.)

2 Trade name of business, if different from name in line 1

3 Executor, trustee, "care of" name

4a Mailing address (street address) (room, apt., or suite no.)

5a Address of business (See instructions.)

4b City, state, and ZIP code

5b City, state, and ZIP code

6 County and state where principal business is located

7 Name of principal officer, grantor, or general partner (See instructions.) ▶

8a Type of entity (Check only one box.) (See instructions.)
- ☐ Individual SSN _____
- ☐ REMIC
- ☐ State/local government
- ☐ Personal service corp.
- ☐ National guard
- ☐ Estate
- ☐ Plan administrator SSN _____
- ☐ Other corporation (specify) _____
- ☐ Federal government/military
- ☐ Trust
- ☐ Partnership
- ☐ Farmers' cooperative
- ☐ Church or church controlled organization
- ☐ Other nonprofit organization (specify) _____ If nonprofit organization enter GEN (if applicable) _____
- ☐ Other (specify) ▶

8b If a corporation, give name of foreign country (if applicable) or state in the U.S. where incorporated ▶

Foreign country	State

9 Reason for applying (Check only one box.)
- ☐ Started new business
- ☐ Hired employees
- ☐ Created a pension plan (specify type) ▶
- ☐ Banking purpose (specify) ▶
- ☐ Changed type of organization (specify) ▶ _____
- ☐ Purchased going business
- ☐ Created a trust (specify) ▶
- ☐ Other (specify) ▶

10 Date business started or acquired (Mo., day, year) (See instructions.)

11 Enter closing month of accounting year. (See instructions.)

12 First date wages or annuities were paid or will be paid (Mo., day, year). **Note:** If applicant is a withholding agent, enter date income will first be paid to nonresident alien. (Mo., day, year) · · · · · · · · · · · · · · · ▶

13 Enter highest number of employees expected in the next 12 months. **Note:** If the applicant does not expect to have any employees during the period, enter "0." · · · · · · · ▶

Nonagricultural	Agricultural	Household

14 Principal activity (See instructions.) ▶

15 Is the principal business activity manufacturing? · · · · · · · · · · · · · · · ☐ Yes ☐ No
If "Yes," principal product and raw material used ▶

16 To whom are most of the products or services sold? Please check the appropriate box. ☐ Business (wholesale)
☐ Public (retail) ☐ Other (specify) ▶ ☐ N/A

17a Has the applicant ever applied for an identification number for this or any other business? · · · · · · · · ☐ Yes ☐ No
Note: If "Yes," please complete lines 17b and 17c.

17b If you checked the "Yes" box in line 17a, give applicant's true name and trade name, if different than name shown on prior application.

True name ▶   Trade name ▶

17c Enter approximate date, city, and state where the application was filed and the previous employer identification number if known.

Approximate date when filed (Mo., day, year)	City and state where filed	Previous EIN

Under penalties of perjury, I declare that I have examined this application, and to the best of my knowledge and belief, it is true, correct, and complete. | Telephone number (include area code)

Name and title (Please type or print clearly.) ▶

Signature ▶   Date ▶

Note: Do not write below this line.   For official use only.

Please leave blank ▶	Geo.	Ind.	Class	Size	Reason for applying

For Paperwork Reduction Act Notice, see attached instructions.   Cat. No. 16055N   Form **SS-4** (Rev. 4-91)

132

General Instructions

(Section references are to the Internal Revenue Code unless otherwise noted.)

Paperwork Reduction Act Notice.—We ask for the information on this form to carry out the Internal Revenue laws of the United States. You are required to give us this information. We need it to ensure that you are complying with these laws and to allow us to figure and collect the right amount of tax.

The time needed to complete and file this form will vary depending on individual circumstances. The estimated average time is:

Recordkeeping	7 min.
Learning about the law or the form	21 min.
Preparing the form	42 min.
Copying, assembling, and sending the form to IRS	20 min.

If you have comments concerning the accuracy of these time estimates or suggestions for making this form more simple, we would be happy to hear from you. You can write to both the **Internal Revenue Service**, Washington, DC 20224, Attention: IRS Reports Clearance Officer, T:FP; and the **Office of Management and Budget**, Paperwork Reduction Project (1545-0003), Washington, DC 20503. **DO NOT** send the tax form to either of these offices. Instead, see **Where To Apply.**

Purpose.—Use Form SS-4 to apply for an employer identification number (EIN). The information you provide on this form will establish your filing requirements.

Who Must File.—You must file this form if you have not obtained an EIN before and

* You pay wages to one or more employees.
* You are required to have an EIN to use on any return, statement, or other document, even if you are not an employer.
* You are required to withhold taxes on income, other than wages, paid to a nonresident alien (individual, corporation, partnership, etc.). For example, individuals who file **Form 1042**, Annual Withholding Tax Return for U.S. Source Income of Foreign Persons, to report alimony paid to nonresident aliens must have EINs.

Individuals who file **Schedule C**, Profit or Loss From Business, or **Schedule F**, Profit or Loss From Farming, of **Form 1040**, U.S. Individual Income Tax Return, must use EINs if they have a Keogh plan or are required to file excise, employment, or alcohol, tobacco, or firearms returns.

The following must use EINs even if they do not have any employees:

* Trusts, except an IRA trust, unless the IRA trust is required to file **Form 990-T**, Exempt Organization Business Income Tax Return, to report unrelated business taxable income or is filing Form 990-T to obtain a refund of the credit from a regulated investment company.
* Estates
* Partnerships
* REMICS (real estate mortgage investment conduits)
* Corporations
* Nonprofit organizations (churches, clubs, etc.)
* Farmers' cooperatives
* Plan administrators

New Business.—If you become the new owner of an existing business, **DO NOT** use the EIN of the former owner. If you already have an EIN, use that number. If you do not have an EIN, apply for one on this form. If you become the "owner" of a corporation by acquiring its stock, use the corporation's EIN.

If you already have an EIN, you may need to get a new one if either the organization or ownership of your business changes. If you incorporate a sole proprietorship or form a partnership, you must get a new EIN. However, **DO NOT** apply for a new EIN if you change only the name of your business.

File Only One Form SS-4.—File only one Form SS-4, regardless of the number of businesses operated or trade names under which a business operates. However, each corporation in an affiliated group must file a separate application.

If you do not have an EIN by the time a return is due, write "Applied for" and the date you applied in the space shown for the number. **DO NOT** show your social security number as an EIN on returns.

If you do not have an EIN by the time a tax deposit is due, send your payment to the Internal Revenue service center for your filing area. (See **Where To Apply** below.) Make your check or money order payable to Internal Revenue Service and show your name (as shown on Form SS-4), address, kind of tax, period covered, and date you applied for an EIN.

For more information about EINs, see **Pub. 583**, Taxpayers Starting a Business.

How To Apply.—You can apply for an EIN either by mail or by telephone. You can get an EIN immediately by calling the Tele-TIN phone number for the service center for your state, or you can send the completed Form SS-4 directly to the service center to receive your EIN in the mail.

Application by Tele-TIN.—The Tele-TIN program is designed to assign EINs by telephone. Under this program, you can receive your EIN over the telephone and use it immediately to file a return or make a payment.

To receive an EIN by phone, complete Form SS-4, then call the Tele-TIN phone number listed for your state under **Where To Apply.** The person making the call must be authorized to sign the form (see **Signature block** on page 3).

An IRS representative will use the information from the Form SS-4 to establish your account and assign you an EIN. Write the number you are given on the upper right-hand corner of the form, sign and date it, and promptly mail it to the Tele-TIN Unit at the service center address for your state.

Application by mail.—Complete Form SS-4 at least 4 to 5 weeks before you will need an EIN. Sign and date the application and mail it to the service center address for your state. You will receive your EIN in the mail in approximately 4 weeks.

Note: *The Tele-TIN phone numbers listed below will involve a long-distance charge to callers outside of the local calling area, and should only be used to apply for an EIN. Use 1-800-829-1040 to ask about an application by mail.*

Where To Apply.—

If your principal business, office or agency, or legal residence in the case of an individual, is located in:	Call the Tele-TIN phone number shown or file with the Internal Revenue service center at:
Florida, Georgia, South Carolina	Atlanta, GA 39901 (404) 455-2360
New Jersey, New York City and counties of Nassau, Rockland, Suffolk, and Westchester	Holtsville, NY 00501 (516) 447-4955
New York (all other counties), Connecticut, Maine, Massachusetts, New Hampshire, Rhode Island, Vermont	Andover, MA 05501 (508) 474-9717
Illinois, Iowa, Minnesota, Missouri, Wisconsin	Kansas City, MO 64999 (816) 926-5999
Delaware, District of Columbia, Maryland, Pennsylvania, Virginia	Philadelphia, PA 19255 (215) 961-3980
Indiana, Kentucky, Michigan, Ohio, West Virginia	Cincinnati, OH 45999 (606) 292-5467
Kansas, New Mexico, Oklahoma, Texas	Austin, TX 73301 (512) 462-7845
Alaska, Arizona, California (counties of Alpine, Amador, Butte, Calaveras, Colusa, Contra Costa, Del Norte, El Dorado, Glenn, Humboldt, Lake, Lassen, Marin, Mendocino, Modoc, Napa, Nevada, Placer, Plumas, Sacramento, San Joaquin, Shasta, Sierra, Siskiyou, Solano, Sonoma, Sutter, Tehama, Trinity, Yolo, and Yuba), Colorado, Idaho, Montana, Nebraska, Nevada, North Dakota, Oregon, South Dakota, Utah, Washington, Wyoming	Ogden, UT 84201 (801) 625-7645
California (all other counties), Hawaii	Fresno, CA 93888 (209) 456-5900
Alabama, Arkansas, Louisiana, Mississippi, North Carolina, Tennessee	Memphis, TN 37501 (901) 365-5970

If you have no legal residence, principal place of business, or principal office or agency in any Internal Revenue District, file your form with the Internal Revenue Service Center, Philadelphia, PA 19255 or call (215) 961-3980.

Specific Instructions

The instructions that follow are for those items that are not self-explanatory. Enter N/A (nonapplicable) on the lines that do not apply.

Line 1.—Enter the legal name of the entity applying for the EIN.

Individuals.—Enter the first name, middle initial, and last name.

Trusts.—Enter the name of the trust.

Estate of a decedent.—Enter the name of the estate.

Partnerships.—Enter the legal name of the partnership as it appears in the partnership agreement.

Corporations.—Enter the corporate name as set forth in the corporation charter or other legal document creating it.

Plan administrators.—Enter the name of the plan administrator. A plan administrator who already has an EIN should use that number.

Line 2.—Enter the trade name of the business if different from the legal name.

Note: *Use the full legal name entered on line 1 on all tax returns to be filed for the entity. However, if a trade name is entered on line 2, use only the name on line 1 or the name on line 2 consistently when filing tax returns.*

Line 3.—Trusts enter the name of the trustee. Estates enter the name of the executor, administrator, or other fiduciary. If the entity applying has a designated person to receive tax information, enter that person's name as the "care of" person. Print or type the first name, middle initial, and last name.

Lines 5a and 5b.—If the physical location of the business is different from the mailing address (lines 4a and 4b), enter the address of the physical location on lines 5a and 5b.

133

Line 7.—Enter the first name, middle initial, and last name of a principal officer if the business is a corporation; of a general partner if a partnership; and of a grantor if a trust.

Line 8a.—Check the box that best describes the type of entity that is applying for the EIN. If not specifically mentioned, check the "other" box and enter the type of entity. Do not enter N/A.

Individual.—Check this box if the individual files Schedule C or F (Form 1040) and has a Keogh plan or is required to file excise, employment, or alcohol, tobacco, or firearms returns. If this box is checked, enter the individual's SSN (social security number) in the space provided.

Plan administrator.—The term plan administrator means the person or group of persons specified as the administrator by the instrument under which the plan is operated. If the plan administrator is an individual, enter the plan administrator's SSN in the space provided.

New withholding agent.—If you are a new withholding agent required to file Form 1042, check the "other" box and enter in the space provided "new withholding agent."

REMICs.—Check this box if the entity is a real estate mortgage investment conduit (REMIC). A REMIC is any entity

1. To which an election to be treated as a REMIC applies for the tax year and all prior tax years,

2. In which all of the interests are regular interests or residual interests,

3. Which has one class of residual interests (and all distributions, if any, with respect to such interests are pro rata),

4. In which as of the close of the 3rd month beginning after the startup date and at all times thereafter, substantially all of its assets consist of qualified mortgages and permitted investments,

5. Which has a tax year that is a calendar year, and

6. With respect to which there are reasonable arrangements designed to ensure that: (a) residual interests are not held by disqualified organizations (as defined in section 860E(e)(5)), and (b) information necessary for the application of section 860E(e) will be made available.

For more information about REMICs see the Instructions for **Form 1066**, U. S. Real Estate Mortgage Investment Conduit Income Tax Return.

Personal service corporations.—Check this box if the entity is a personal service corporation. An entity is a personal service corporation for a tax year only if

1. The entity is a C corporation for the tax year.

2. The principal activity of the entity during the testing period (as defined in Temporary Regulations section 1.441-4T(f)) for the tax year is the performance of personal service.

3. During the testing period for the tax year, such services are substantially performed by employee-owners.

4. The employee-owners own 10 percent of the fair market value of the outstanding stock in the entity on the last day of the testing period for the tax year.

For more information about personal service corporations, see the instructions to Form 1120, U.S. Corporation Income Tax Return, and Temporary Regulations section 1.441-4T.

Other corporations.—This box is for any corporation other than a personal service corporation. If you check this box, enter the type of corporation (such as insurance company) in the space provided.

Other nonprofit organizations.—Check this box if the nonprofit organization is other than a church or church-controlled organization and specify the type of nonprofit organization (for example, an educational organization.)

Group exemption number (GEN).—If the applicant is a nonprofit organization that is a subordinate organization to be included in a group exemption letter under Revenue Procedure 80-27, 1980-1 C.B. 677, enter the GEN in the space provided. If you do not know the GEN, contact the parent organization for it. GEN is a four-digit number. Do not confuse it with the nine-digit EIN.

Line 9.—Check only one box. Do not enter N/A.

Started new business.—Check this box if you are starting a new business that requires an EIN. If you check this box, enter the type of business being started. **DO NOT** apply if you already have an EIN and are only adding another place of business.

Changed type of organization.—Check this box if the business is changing its type of organization, for example, if the business was a sole proprietorship and has been incorporated or has become a partnership. If you check this box, specify in the space provided the type of change made, for example, "from sole proprietorship to partnership."

Purchased going business.—Check this box if you acquired a business through purchase. Do not use the former owner's EIN. If you already have an EIN, use that number.

Hired employees.—Check this box if the existing business is requesting an EIN because it has hired or is hiring employees and is therefore required to file employment tax return for which an EIN is required. **DO NOT** apply if you already have an EIN and are only hiring employees.

Created a trust.—Check this box if you created a trust, and enter the type of trust created.

Created a pension plan.—Check this box if you have created a pension plan and need this number for reporting purposes. Also, enter the type of plan created.

Banking purpose.—Check this box if you are requesting an EIN for banking purpose only and enter the banking purpose (for example, checking, loan, etc.).

Other (specify).—Check this box if you are requesting an EIN for any reason other than those for which there are checkboxes and enter the reason.

Line 10.—If you are starting a new business, enter the starting date of the business. If the business you acquired is already operating, enter the date you acquired the business. Trusts should enter the date the trust was legally created. Estates should enter the date of death of the decedent whose name appears on line 1.

Line 11.—Enter the last month of your accounting year or tax year. An accounting year or tax year is usually 12 consecutive months. It may be a calendar year or a fiscal year (including a period of 52 or 53 weeks). A calendar year is 12 consecutive months ending on December 31. A fiscal year is either 12 consecutive months ending on the last day of any month other than December or a 52-53 week year. For more information

on accounting periods, see **Pub. 538**, Accounting Periods and Methods.

Individuals.—Your tax year generally will be a calendar year.

Partnerships.—Partnerships generally should conform to the tax year of either (1) its majority partners; (2) its principal partners; (3) the tax year that results in the least aggregate deferral of income (see Temporary Regulations section 1.706-1T); or (4) some other tax year, if (a) a business purpose is established for the fiscal year, or (b) the fiscal year is a "grandfather" year, or (c) an election is made under section 444 to have a fiscal year. (See the Instructions for **Form 1065**, U.S. Partnership Return of Income, for more information.)

REMICs.—Remics must have a calendar year as their tax year.

Personal service corporations.—A personal service corporation generally must adopt a calendar year unless:

1. It can establish to the satisfaction of the Commissioner that there is a business purpose for having a different tax year, or

2. It elects under section 444 to have a tax year other than a calendar year.

Line 12.—If the business has or will have employees, enter on this line the date on which the business began or will begin to pay wages to the employees. If the business does not have any plans to have employees, enter N/A on this line.

New withholding agent.—Enter the date you began or will begin to pay income to a nonresident alien. This also applies to individuals who are required to file Form 1042 to report alimony paid to a nonresident alien.

Line 14.—Generally, enter the exact type of business being operated (for example, advertising agency, farm, labor union, real estate agency, steam laundry, rental of coin-operated vending machine, investment club, etc.).

Governmental.—Enter the type of organization (state, county, school district, or municipality, etc.)

Nonprofit organization (other than governmental).—Enter whether organized for religious, educational, or humane purposes, and the principal activity (for example, religious organization—hospital, charitable).

Mining and quarrying.—Specify the process and the principal product (for example, mining bituminous coal, contract drilling for oil, quarrying dimension stone, etc.).

Contract construction.—Specify whether general contracting or special trade contracting. Also, show the type of work normally performed (for example, general contractor for residential buildings, electrical subcontractor, etc.).

Trade.—Specify the type of sales and the principal line of goods sold (for example, wholesale dairy products, manufacturer's representative for mining machinery, retail hardware, etc.).

Manufacturing.—Specify the type of establishment operated (for example, sawmill, vegetable cannery, etc.).

Signature block.—The application must be signed by: (1) the individual, if the person is an individual, (2) the president, vice president, or other principal officer, if the person is a corporation, (3) a responsible and duly authorized member or officer having knowledge of its affairs, if the person is a partnership or other unincorporated organization, or (4) the fiduciary, if the person is a trust or estate.

Trainer Log Sheet

Trainer Name _____   Week Starting _____

Date	Time	Client	Comments

Index

Thousands Of Personal Trainers Are Using Computers To Manage Their Businesses. Shouldn't You?

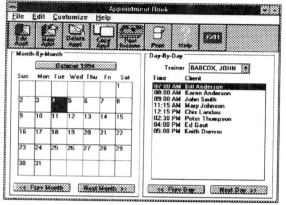

Manage your personal training business better with less time and effort!

Item #	Item	Price
2002	PTBM Standard Edition	$69.95 + $2.50 S&H
3003	PTBM Club Edition	$249.95

SYSTEM REQUIREMENTS: An IBM-compatible computer with a 386, 486, or Pentium processor with Microsoft Windows 3.1 or Windows 95. Does not support Machintosh computers.

It's easy to see why *Personal Trainer Business Manager for Windows*, the best-selling software for managing a personal training business, is used by over several thousand personal trainers, gyms, and health clubs to manage their personal training businesses. Not only does *Personal Trainer Business Manager for Windows* save these personal trainers time. It allows them to manage their businesses better.

Here are just some of the things you will be able to do with *Personal Trainer Business Manager for Windows*:

* Schedule client training sessions for any number of clients
* Automatically keep track of what clients owe
* Print client invoices and past due statements
* Record client medical histories
* Maintain client training logs
* Print reports and graphs of client progress
* Record training income
* Track income and expenses
* Generate income, expense, and profit and loss reports and graphs
* Maintain a database of clients
* Create client mailing lists
* Print frequently used personal trainer business forms
* Manage up to four other trainers

*NOTE: The Club Edition includes all the features of the Standard Edition plus it supports an unlimited number of trainers, networking, and security.

Personal Trainer
BUSINESS MANAGER
for Windows

Software for Managing

ONLY $69.95

Now There Is Also A Quick And Easy Way To Schedule Fitness Classes

Fitness Class Scheduler for Windows simplifies the task of scheduling fitness classes and keeping track of fitness instructors. With *Fitness Class Scheduler for Windows*, you will be able to create better class schedules with less time and effort. Here are just some of the things you will be able to do with *Fitness Class Scheduler for Windows*:

* Schedule and reschedule classes simply by arranging them on the screen
* Maintain separate schedules for each room and location
* Keep track of instructor names, addresses, and telephone numbers
* Record the days and times each instructor is available
* Automatically display lists of available instructors
* Quickly find an available substitute instructor
* Print individual schedules for each instructor
* Print complete class schedules for students
* Create reports of hours and classes taught by each instructor
* Easily customize a schedule's appearance to suit your needs

Microsoft, Windows, and Windows 95 are either trademarks or registered trademarks of Microsoft Corporation. IBM is a registered trademark of International Business Machines. Personal Trainer Business Manager and Fitness Class Scheduler are trademarks of Gaucas, Inc.

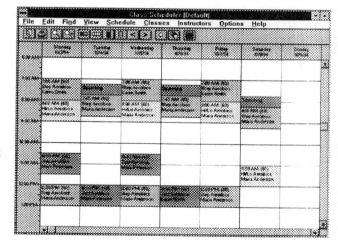

Item #	Item	Price
4004	Fitness Class Scheduler	$149.95

SYSTEM REQUIREMENTS: An IBM-compatible computer with a 386, 486, or Pentium processor with Microsoft Windows 3.1 or Windows 95. Does not support Machintosh computers.

To Order Call 1-800-823-3488 Ext 225